How to Be a Christian and Still Enjoy Life

FRITZ RIDENOUR

Author of the best-seller "How to Be a Christian Without Being Religious"

Regal Books

A Division of GL Publications
Ventura, California, U.S.A.

Published by Regal Books
A Division of GL Publications
Ventura, California 93006
Printed in U.S.A.

Any omission of credits or permissions granted is unintentional. The publisher
requests documentation for future printings.

Library of Congress Cataloging-in-Publication Data

Ridenour, Fritz.
     How to be a Christian and still enjoy life.

     Includes bibliographies.
     1. Christian life—1960-   I. Title.
BV4501.2.R515   1988   248.4   88-11395
ISBN 0-8307-1218-6

1 2 3 4 5 6 7 8 9 10/ 91 90 89 88

Rights for publishing this book in other languages are contracted by Gospel
Literature International (GLINT) foundation. GLINT also provides technical
help for the adaptation, translation, and publishing of Bible study resources
and books in scores of languages worldwide. For further information, contact
GLINT, Post Office Box 488, Rosemead, California, 91770, U.S.A., or the
publisher.

TO MY TUESDAY NIGHT CARE GROUP, FELLOW STRUGGLERS WITH VALUES.

CONTENTS

PREFACE
HOW TO GET THE MOST FROM THIS LIFETOUCH BOOK

Welcome to what I hope becomes an exciting and different adventure in reading and learning. In a way, this book is an experiment in cooperative discovery. It combines my comments and insights as an author with your study of Scripture as you look up references, interact with God's Word and write down what it means to you.

I've tried to construct this values study of Philippians so it can be used in three different ways, depending on how much time you choose to spend on it.

The least demanding method is to read each chapter for information and inspiration and skip the LifeTouch Department questions. This is only a first step toward getting full value from the book, so I hope you will want to go further.

A second and much more effective approach is to read each chapter, then interact with the LifeTouch Department questions on your own as you do further thinking and praying about the Christian value being discussed. For best results, keep a journal/notebook of some kind to record your observations, feelings and discoveries from Scripture.

Be sure to try some of the suggestions under *Taking Stock and Setting Goals*. One of the major weaknesses of most Christian reading and study is that there is no practical follow-through. As chapter 9 points out, hearing and seeing are important ways to learn, but *what we do we become.*

Are you wondering why you aren't making more spiritual progress? Why you hear sermon after sermon or sit in lesson after lesson, but you don't see much change in the way you act or respond to stress and problems? Part of the answer is that we all grow at different rates, but a major hurdle is that we don't always apply what we think we know.

An athlete doesn't become proficient in his or her sport by simply reading about it or listening to a lecture and then not bothering to practice or play a real game. It takes many hours to develop a good backhand or backstroke. It takes practice to become proficient at typing, operating a computer or driving a car. The principle is so obvious it needs no embellishment. Why then don't we use it more as we seek to "grow up into Christ"? (Eph. 4:15, *NEB*).

As chapter 5 points out, God is at work within us, but we are to work out our salvation in specific, nitty-gritty, even mundane, ways. Simply understanding a principle from Scripture is not enough. If it is to become a true value, we have to do it—in even the tiniest, simplest way—or it remains only another wonderful truth or law that we know but don't really use. The Pharisees knew over 600 of these wonderful truths and Jesus called them the Pharisees "whited sepulchres" (Matt. 23:27, *KJV*).

A third way to use this book, which I believe would give the best results, is by studying it in a discussion group that meets weekly, or, at least, on some consistent basis. Have one regular leader or share leadership among different members of your group. A leader's guide, published separately, provides more than enough material for each session plan, and you can use what works best for you and your group.

Keep in mind that the session plans are designed to make maximum use of the discussion method of teaching and learning. They are not designed for a "master lecturer" who desires to spoon-feed a group the results of his or her hours of careful study. A major goal is to have everyone in the group prepare for each session by reading the chapter and related Scripture references for that session, completing the LifeTouch questions and coming to the session ready to participate by asking questions and sharing insights.

Naturally, I hope you will use methods two and three to get the most from this study. But, whatever method you choose, I'd like to hear from you. Write me in care of the publisher with your comments, ideas or suggestions. My goal is to create a tool through which God's Word can touch you in new and different ways, as you search the Scriptures to discover what He has especially for you.

Fritz Ridenour
Canyon Country, CA
1988

INTRODUCTION
Values Speak Louder Than Words

*T*he old saying has it that "What you do speaks so loudly I can't hear what you say." The apostle Paul isn't credited with making this remark, but I'm sure he would have agreed with it. To read any of Paul's Epistles—letters—is to take a course in Christian values. Paul taught doctrine—what Christians believe—but he always went beyond beliefs, to values—how Christians should act and live.

Paul never confused beliefs with values; he blended them. For Paul, a value was a principle or belief that was so important it actually affected what he did—how he lived.

Paul was someone who lived from the inside out. If our beliefs are inside—and truly a part of us—they will come out, sooner or later. For example, we say we believe in love, but when and where do we act lovingly? We say we believe in commitment, but do we show up on time, if at all?

Turning our beliefs into actual values—things we do—is not something we learn in one lesson, or even one lifetime. It's a process of growth toward godliness that includes:

1. Discovering (or getting taught) what is important. Learning principles, morals, doctrines, beliefs.

2. Learning to make these beliefs part of you and your personality—who you really are.

3. Choosing from many daily opportunities to act on these beliefs.

4. Living from the inside out—doing what you say you believe to be true.[1]

In many of his letters, Paul worked out this process in a very deliberate, formal way (see, for example, Romans Galatians Ephesians or Colossians). But in a very brief and informal "thank-you note" to his friends in Philippi, Paul teaches a short course in Christian values without really setting out to do so. And that's what makes Philippians so valuable. Christian values just pop out from everywhere and teach us what is truly important and how we should live.

Paul wouldn't have been too impressed by today's new view that says values are simply beliefs, opinions or things that may be important to a certain individual, and all you can do is try to help that person clarify what his or her values are. Values clarification is a major teaching tool in the secular, humanist movement led by such scholars as Dr. Sidney B. Simon at the University of Massachusetts, who believes in a process that helps people arrive at an answer, but not necessarily by believing any ultimate set of values. According to Dr. Simon, values clarification "is a methodology to help you make a decision, to act, to determine what has meaning for you."[2]

The traditional view of values says there are eternal, everlasting, never changing truths and principles by which we should live and pass on or transfer from one generation to another. But, Dr. Simon claims that these eternal truths

God's eternal truths do not change with each passing fad or philosophy.

have become encrusted with ritual and tradition and are being transferred ineffectually across a values gap of radically diverse views and opinions. Paul and the writers of Scripture, however, had no values gap. Moved by the Holy Spirit, they put down the great truths that were to last forever (see Isa. 48:8; Heb. 13:8; 1 Pet. 1:25).

As a follower of Christ, you can use both views of values to grow in your faith. There are eternal truths to be learned from the Word of God and these truths do not change with each passing fad or philosophy, secular humanism included. At the same time, Christians need to clarify just what their biblical values really are. They need to identify what is to be important to them as well as what is really important to God. Are they valuing God's Word or are they valuing the wisdom of a worldly system that often decides what is right or wrong on the basis of the latest trend or what seems to be working for the most people?

Above all, the Christian has to ask, Am I actually living by what I say I believe? Am I applying all those wonderful truths that I read in Scripture or hear preached from the pulpit and to which I nod assent every Sunday?

Paul Practiced What He Valued

In the chapters that follow, we will look at 10 of Paul's values—ways of living that he actually practiced. He practiced them so well he could say, "My brothers I should like you all to imitate me and observe those whose lives are based on the pattern that we give you" (Phil. 3:17, *Phillips*).

Paul could make such a bold statement only because he knew he wasn't strong enough to stand by himself. That's why he shares that when he is weak, then he is strong, because God's strength is made perfect in his weakness (see 2 Cor. 12:9,10). When he writes his letter to the Philippians, Paul is weak indeed, chained to a Roman guard and awaiting possible execution, yet his values pop out in almost every paragraph:

> *Paul valued praise and thanksgiving,* and that's one reason why Philippians is often called the Epistle of joy (see Phil. 1:4, 3:1, 4:4).
>
> *Paul valued love and spiritual insight* that would bear fruit in wisdom and purity (see 1:9-11).
>
> *Paul valued commitment and discipline—* for him each day was an opportunity to live for Christ (see 1:21).

Paul valued unity and humility and often demonstrated how they go together (see 2:2,3).

Paul valued integrity as he worked out his salvation while God worked within him (see 2:12,13).

Paul valued righteousness in Christ and he counted all other things worthless in comparison (see 3:8,9).

Paul valued perseverance and goal setting and always pressed on toward the ultimate goal—Christ Himself (see 3:12-14).

Paul valued prayer and used it as a prescription to conquer worry and anxiety (see 4:6,7).

Paul valued sound thinking that focused on what is true, honest, right, pure, lovely, admirable, excellent and praiseworthy (see 4:8).

Paul valued success and contentment, but only on God's terms. He knew he could do anything God wanted him to do as God supplied all his needs from His riches in glory through Christ (see 4:13,19).

Do You Want Joy or Happiness?

Paul had many other values, of course, but as we study those mentioned above, we should find a valuable bonus in a working definition of the word *joy*. By working definition, I mean one that works in your life. Many Christians confuse joy with "happiness" or "having a continually good time." If the job is going well, a raise is on the horizon, all the children are getting excellent grades in school and that demon slice is finally being exorcised from our golf swing, then we think we are enjoying life.

Paul will show us that joy lies in taking our beliefs into the realm of values and living them from the inside out. Almost every paragraph of Philippians teaches that joy has little to do with feeling elated, euphoric, amused, full of glee or satisfied with life in general. No one speaks more about joy and rejoicing than Paul. In fact, in his letter to Philippi, he uses the words 17 times. We almost forget that as he is writing he is in the slammer—on death row—hardly a happy scene.

How can Paul talk about joy and rejoicing? Has he finally cracked after putting on all that missionary mileage? Is he merely mouthing religious platitudes to keep up his flagging spirits while Nero decides to behead him or let him go? Or is the apostle Paul's joy something very real, a value that can touch our lives and breathe new energy into the safe, secure and sometimes dull routine we call being a Christian? Paul invites us to read his letter to the Philippians for ourselves and discover with him what it means to live and still enjoy life.

The following questions are designed for your personal study or to discuss with a group. Record your answers in your journal/notebook.

1. According to this chapter, a belief or doctrine is _____, but a value is _____. What is more important, right beliefs or right actions?

2. Review the four-step process of growth that turns

beliefs into values that are practiced daily. Why does this process take time—sometimes a lifetime?

3. When you hear the word *value*, what do you think of? List three Christian values that are very important to you.

4. What can you learn from Paul about the difference between joy and being happy? If happiness depends upon things going right, upon what does joy depend?

Taking Stock and Setting Goals

1. Take the following spiritual values inventory to see where you want to progress in the 10 categories below. Circle a number from 1 to 10 (1 meaning weak; 10, strong). After finishing your study of values based on Philippians, you will have the opportunity to take this same inventory again to see how you have grown in the following categories:

Thanking and praising God   1 2 3 4 5 6 7 8 9 10

Becoming more loving   1 2 3 4 5 6 7 8 9 10

Developing stronger commitments   1 2 3 4 5 6 7 8 9 10

Becoming more humble, a team player 1 2 3 4 5 6 7 8 9 10

Developing stronger integrity   1 2 3 4 5 6 7 8 9 10

Appreciating righteousness in Christ   1 2 3 4 5 6 7 8 9 10

Learning how to persevere   1 2 3 4 5 6 7 8 9 10

Handling anxiety and stress   1 2 3 4 5 6 7 8 9 10

Sound spiritual thinking   1 2 3 4 5 6 7 8 9 10

Understanding true success   1 2 3 4 5 6 7 8 9 10

2. How much do you know about Paul's background? For how he was changed from Saul, the Pharisee, to Paul the Apostle, see Acts chapters 7 and 9. For how he started a church in Philippi, read Acts 16. Also, read the entire letter of Philippians in different versions each day during the coming week.

Notes
1. Larry Richards and Norm Wakefield, *Basic Christian Values* (Grand Rapids, MI: Zondervan Publishing House, 1974), p. 34.
2. Sydney B. Simon, *Meeting Yourself Halfway* (Allen, TX: Argus Communications, 1974), p. xiii.

CHAPTER ONE
THE PEOPLE WHO ENJOY LIFE MOST

$\mathbb{D}$o most people you know enjoy life by consuming and collecting? Or is their enjoyment centered around celebrating and praising?

Consumers and collectors are not hard to spot. Television commercials pound away 24 hours a day teaching us to be connoisseurs of good times, fast food and bargains that promise happiness. In one sense, we are all *de facto* consumers and collectors, because we live in a society that could not survive without us. Furthermore, we have been brainwashed to believe we cannot survive without all the "stuff" society says we must consume.

But what is a celebrator? When you hear the word *celebration*, what comes to mind? Party time? Winning the championship? Or do celebrators have a special approach to life that sets them apart from consumers and collectors?

The Star Thrower Knew the Secret

In his haunting essay, "The Star Thrower," naturalist Loren Eiseley tells of walking on the beach at dawn following a storm. Tourists and professional shellers roam over the sand in greedy competition. By dawn's early light they scramble over the rocks and wade through tidal pools, accumulating sacks and buckets of starfish and all types of shells, many of which still house living creatures. They dump their prizes into iron kettles provided by the nearby resort hotels and boil the shells—and their occupants—to clean them up and make them ready for sale or proud display on mantles back home.

As Eiseley proceeds on his walk through the grey dawn, he sees in the distance what appears to be a man who stoops, picks something up off the beach and flings it out to sea. Eventually Eiseley reaches the figure and sees him quickly and gently scoop up another starfish. He sails it beyond the breakers, muttering softly, "It may live if the offshore pull is strong enough."

Suddenly embarrassed, Eiseley asks the star thrower, "Do you collect?"

"Only for the living," is his answer, and he stoops to scoop up another starfish that has washed upon the beach to face certain death, as the tide recedes and the sun bakes the sand. Again, he flings a starfish into deeper water so it might live another day, another week or even longer.

In one sense the star thrower's task is hopeless. He can save only a few of the thousands of creatures perishing around him. But the numbers don't matter. Instead of collecting starfish and other "trophies" to gather dust on his mantle, the star thrower prefers to give life another chance.

"The stars throw well," he says. "One can help them."[1]

The star thrower knew the secret. Can we?

Dr. Denis Waitley is a behavioral psychologist and specialist in stress management and human potential who has counseled Viet Nam POWs, Iranian hostages, Olympic athletes and Apollo moon program astronauts. He writes:

> Life cannot be collected. Happiness cannot be traveled to, owned, earned, worn or consumed. Happiness is the spiritual experience of

living every minute with love, grace and gratitude. The gift of life is not a treasure hunt . . . .
The secret is to turn a life of collection into a life
of celebration. [2]

Letter from a First-Century Star Thrower

Down through the years there have been people who have
learned the secret of celebrating. One of the greatest celebrators of all was the apostle Paul, who spent the better
part of his life rejoicing in what he called "the good news."
Everywhere he went, Paul celebrated and sang praises to
God, but it hadn't always been that way. Earlier in life he
was called Saul and his favorite pastime was persecuting
members of a sect that followed the teachings of Jesus,
the Nazarene, a radical troublemaker who had gotten His
just deserts on a Roman gibbet outside the wall of Jerusa-
lem.

In his Pharisee days, Saul was a collector, not of
things, but of power and prestige. He basked in the admir-
ing looks of fellow legalists who would say, "There goes
Saul, a real Hebrew of the Hebrews. He can trace his pedigree back to the tribe of Benjamin. He practices the law
perfectly. How I wish I had his discipline!"

Saul strides onto the pages of Scripture in Acts chapter
7 when he holds the coats of those who stone Stephen for
his Christian beliefs. Then he leaves for Damascus to find
more Christians and throw them into prison. But somewhere on that road he suddenly finds himself flat on his
back, staring into a blinding light and hearing a voice ask,
"Saul, Saul, why are you giving me such a bad time?" (see
Acts 9:4).

The voice belonged to Jesus, the very name Paul was
trying to blot from existence. In order to change the way

Saul saw things, Jesus struck him blind for a few days so he could think it over. When his sight returned, Saul saw life in a totally different way. Now he counted all of his trophies as rubbish. He realized that righteousness doesn't come through obeying laws, it comes through faith in Christ.

Saul the collector became Paul, celebrator of the good news. Paul could even celebrate while doing time in a Roman prison for his belief in Christ, and that's where we find him as he opens a letter to some Christian friends in Philippi, a bustling trade center several hundred miles away.

As Paul writes to the Philippians, he is in the twilight of a career that has included three missionary journeys across the then-known civilized world, and the planting of churches in key centers of population, like Philippi. But now he is in prison in Rome, chained to one of Caesar's praetorian guards and facing possible execution.

Paul's situation is bleak. Nonetheless, some of his first words are, "All my prayers for you are full of praise to God!" (Phil. 1:3, *TLB*). One reason Paul begins on such a joyful note is that his friends in Philippi have just sent him a care package and some much needed words of encouragement. It makes Paul happy just to remember how he met the Philippian believers and how they have been his partners in spreading the gospel "from the first day until now" (v. 5).

Paul calls the Philippians "partners" for some very good reasons. They are the only body of believers named in the New Testament from whom he actually accepted any gift of help (see 4:15-17). Paul had a strict rule about not taking handouts. He was a tent maker (see Acts 18:3), who "worked night and day in order not to be a burden to anyone" while preaching the gospel to them (1 Thess.

2:9). For Paul to accept help from the Philippians means there was something very special between them.

But the bedrock reason for Paul's joy is not friendship with the Philippians, deep and special as that friendship was. Friends, after all, can change, become offended and drop you, or just get busy and drift away. Paul's joy depended squarely on his relationship to Jesus Christ. Because he knew Christ personally, Paul could "rejoice in the Lord always" (see Phil. 3:1, 4:4). He knew what it was to be a front-runner and he knew something about the agony of defeat. And through it all he rejoiced—and thanked God.

Is the Root of All Sin Thanklessness?

Linked inseparably to praise and rejoicing are thankfulness and gratitude. I tend to agree that a good case could be made for the idea that thanklessness is the root of all sin, but that a thankful heart is the parent of all other virtues. Popular Christian opinion says that pride is the root of all sin, but think of how the serpent got Eve to walk the primrose path to the forbidden tree and take that first ill-fated bite. What made her vulnerable to his appeal to her pride and the tantalizing possibility of being "like God, knowing good and evil"? (Gen. 3:4). Surely ingratitude was right there at the center of Eve's soul saying, "Yes, God's done a lot for me, but is it enough?" Ingratitude always concludes that enough is never enough.

And when I lack gratitude, I center on myself and pride controls my thoughts. It is hard to be proud and thankful at the same time—unless you are thankful because God made you so much better, prettier and smarter than anyone else! But whether thanklessness leads to pride or vice versa is not our main concern. Let's get back to Paul and

learn more about what leads to joy and rejoicing. Perhaps
C. S. Lewis had Paul in mind when he observed that the
people who praise most are those who enjoy life most.

Do you think Lewis was right? If so, what did Lewis
mean? Did he mean that I praise and thank God because I
am enjoying life, or did he mean I enjoy life because I
always remember to thank God and praise Him for His
blessings?

Perhaps he meant a little bit of both. Somebody has
said that we aren't made happy by what we have but by
what we are thankful for. If you doubt this, just ask any
parent on the day after Christmas, when all those brightly
wrapped, eagerly anticipated gifts have turned into a used
toy lot.

And adults are no different. I talked with a friend not
long after the holidays and he mentioned how he and his
family have beaten those Christmas blues, which seem to
set in around 11:00 A.M. on December 25. It's after all the
presents have been opened, and eyes start feeling grainy
from lack of sleep, while an already overtaxed stomach
wearily prepares for another onslaught of calories, com-
monly known as Christmas dinner.

But in this case, Ed, his wife and his college-age son
and daughter, postponed their own Christmas dinner and
helped others have one instead. They all went down to a
restaurant operated by a Christian friend who makes it his
annual custom to be open on Christmas Day to feed needy
families. Ed's family had a great time waiting on tables for
three hours; they went home feeling a different kind of
Christmas joy.

"It was nothing really that dramatic," Ed told me. "But
I know that it helped us appreciate Christmas rather than
just be bored spectators. We were doing something for the
holiday rather than letting the holiday do something for us.

DO YOU
REACH OUT?
OR
TAKE IN?

We were giving, rather than watching Christmas happen one more time."

Why Not Fine-tune Your Praise Perspective?

Ed's simple Christmas story clearly illustrates the difference between collecting and consuming or celebrating with praise and gratitude. One leads to jaded boredom, simply accumulating more and more and living less and less. But the other leads to joy as you appreciate more and more while wanting—and needing—less and less.

Viktor Frankl, the developer of logotherapy (that which focuses on man's search for meaning), survived years of torture in Nazi death camps by deciding that his persecutors could strip him of everything except his power to decide how he would react to the situation. Frankl survived while his father, mother, brother and wife died in the camps or were sent to gas ovens. Only his sister survived along with him.

Frankl did his best to help his fellow prisoners, but more and more of them died as they lost hope. He comments that what they really needed was a fundamental change in attitude toward life. They had to learn that "it did not really matter what we expected from life, but rather what life expected from us."[3]

Paul would agree, but would be sure to add, "What *Christ* expects from me." Paul was so full of praise and gratitude that his life was one big experience of reaching out instead of taking in.

And what of us? Is praise simply a belief or a doctrine? Something we agree is good and right and that we should do regularly? Or are praise and gratitude true values that we practice every day?

How do we begin to develop the same kind of praise

WHEN LIFE GIVES YOU LEMONS, WHAT DO YOU DO?

perspective that Paul had? We can start by gauging all of our activities by one simple question: Is what I'm doing putting me on the side of the collectors and consumers, or am I celebrating my relationship to Jesus Christ?

Granted, it won't be easy. Perspective is not changed as easily as a shirt or a skirt, but it can happen. In a Christmas letter to her friends and family, author Pat Rushford wrote about never ceasing to marvel at "our Lord's ability to turn lemons into lemonade." She referred to a poem she included in her fine book, *What Kids Need Most in a Mom.* Its words aptly explain how God can change the bitter to the sweet:

He gives me hope in hopeless situations,
And helps me see the rainbow
On the other side of rain.
He heals the thorn infested wounds
That I might smell the roses.
He gives me tears to wash away the pain;
O, but then . . . then . . .
He gives me joy so I can laugh again.[4]

But What If I Don't *Feel* Joyful?

"But what if I don't *feel* like laughing or praising God?" you
may ask. "Won't I be a phony if I praise Him when things
are a total mess?"

Surely Paul would say no. Like Viktor Frankl, he was
stripped of everything except what went on inside his
heart and soul. But Paul knew praise is something you
have to do within while you are doing without. Though he
was doing without freedom, friends and decent food, he
could still *choose to rejoice*, even if he didn't feel like it.
Instead of bemoaning what life had done *to* him, Paul
remembered all the things God was doing *for* him, and his
joy conquered his circumstances.

Paul has much to teach us about the difference
between true joy and being happy because things are
going right. If our joy depends on having everything go
right, we are fair game for the TV hucksters who tell us:
"Just send me $25, brothers and sisters! I'll mail you this
special prayer shawl and guarantee God will give you
health, wealth and blessings above anything you can ask or
think!"

Sad to say, this kind of drivel is broadcast over the air-
waves every day and thousands of dollars pour in from

INSTEAD OF
BEMOANING WHAT
LIFE IS DOING
TO YOU,
REMEMBER
ALL THE THINGS
GOD IS DOING
FOR YOU.

trusting souls who are trying to bribe God. This isn't praise; it is spiritual pornography.

We do not praise God in order to get His guarantee that we will be well, rich or out of debt. But in praising and thanking God with no strings attached, we let down our defenses and give ourselves to Him. The result is that we allow God to give more of Himself to us. *He* makes the lemons into lemonade. *He* is our source of true joy.

The following questions are designed for your personal study or to discuss with a group. Record your answers in your journal/notebook.

1. What does the story of the star thrower say to you? Was the star thrower wasting his time? Why or why not?

2. Reread the statement by Dr. Denis Waitley in this chapter. Why can't happiness be collected, traveled to, owned, earned, worn or consumed? How do you turn a life of collection into a life of celebration?

3. In Philippians 1:4, Paul mentions that he always prays with joy when he thinks of his friends in Philippi. In Philippians 3:1 and 4:4 he urges them to rejoice again and again. Do you think Christians of the first century were more joyful than Christians today? Should there be more praying with joy among believers today? How about your church or group? How about you?

4. Which of the following Scripture references touch you personally and inspire you to rejoice more often in any circumstance? Write down your observations and feelings: Deuteronomy 12:7, Psalm 5:11, 33:1, Zechariah 9:9 (compare Matt. 21:1-11), Luke 10:20, Romans 12:15, 1 Thessalonians 5:16-18.

5. Why should Paul's words about rejoicing in any situation be familiar to the Philippians? How had Paul modeled this for them years before? (see Acts 16).

6. Do you agree or disagree that "thanklessness is the root of all sin"? Read the account of how the serpent seduced Eve in the garden (see Gen. 3:1-6). What are some key phrases that reveal his strategy? Why would wisdom be so appealing to Eve?

7. Do you agree or disagree with C. S. Lewis when he said that the people who praise most are those who enjoy life most? How does his comment compare to the idea that "we aren't made happy by what we have but by what we are thankful for"?

8. The story of how Ed and his family beat the Christmas blues contains a key truth. What is it? Have you ever experienced Christmas blues because children—or adults—didn't seem to appreciate their gifts or all the other work you did to shop, decorate, clean and cook?

Taking Stock and Setting Goals

1. I am least thankful and joyful when:

2. I am most thankful and joyful when:

3. Some areas where I need to think about doing less consuming and collecting are:

4. Some areas where I can celebrate life by praising and thanking God more are:

Lord, I just want to praise you

Help me realize it is not what I have but what I appreciate that counts. Keep me from the sin of thanklessness. Fill my life with gratitude until it bubbles over with praise and thanksgiving as I live from the inside out.

Notes
1. Loren Eiseley, *The Star Thrower* (New York: Times Books, Div. of Quadrangle/The New York Times Books Co., Inc. 1979), p. 172.
2. Denis E. Waitley, *The Seeds of Greatness* (Old Tappan, NJ: Fleming H. Revell Co., 1983), p. 218.
3. Viktor Frankl, *Man's Search for Meaning* (New York: Pocket Books, Div. of Simon & Schuster, Inc., original © 1959, 1984 edition), p. 98.
4. Pat Rushford, *What Kids Need Most in a Mom* (Old Tappan, NJ: Fleming H. Revell Co., 1986), pp. 137,138. Used by permission.

CHAPTER TWO
YOUR LOVE BANK NEVER CLOSES

Personal Savings and Loan

OPEN

Without a doubt, the apostle Paul was one of the most cogent thinkers the world has ever known. His letters comprise a major part of the New Testament and are the basis for much of Christian theology. Some of his best writing, perhaps, is in his prayers for the saints, and in Philippians 1:9-11 we find just such a prayer. In one typically long sentence, Paul describes the mature love and insight that is the bedrock of a life of joy for the Christian:

> And this is my prayer: that your love may abound more and more in knowledge and depth of insight, so that you may be able to discern what is best and may be pure and blameless until the day of Christ, filled with the fruit of righteousness that comes through Jesus Christ—to the glory and praise of God.

When describing the marks of a mature church—or a mature Christian—Paul seldom fails to include love. His favorite trio of Christian values is faith, hope and love and he often mentions them in one breath. For example, see 1 Thessalonians 1:3 and Colossians 1:3-6. Or try Paul's ringing conclusion to the love chapter, 1 Corinthians 13: "And now these three remain: faith, hope and love. But the greatest of these is love" (v. 13).

But as Paul begins his letter to the Philippian church, he mentions only love. Why didn't Paul think it necessary to mention faith and hope to the Philippians? In 1 Corinthians 13:7 he strongly implies that mature love always trusts—has faith—and always hopes. Apparently Paul was convinced that the Philippians had already been practicing love at a very mature level because he prays that their love might abound "more and more" at the same level of maturity they had already demonstrated.

But what is mature love, in a biblical sense? It might be better to say that love in the biblical sense is always mature. The most used Greek word (over 300 times) for love in the New Testament is *agape*, which reaches far beyond love between friends—*phileo* or romantic love—*eros*.

Eros love and phileo love are based on *quid pro quo*—something for something. Both depend on reciprocal feelings—you love me and I'll love you back. Agape love, however, is selfless, unconditional and demands nothing in return.

The Bible never commands Christians to have strong feelings of friendship or romance for each other. It does, however, command all Christians to practice agape love. Jesus laid down that command at the Last Supper when He told His disciples, "A new command I give you: Love one another. As I have loved you, so you must love one another" (John 13:34). The apostle John reminds us of this command in his first Epistle, "And this is his command: to believe in the name of his Son, Jesus Christ, and to love one another as he commanded us" (1 John 3:23).

There are countless stories of agape love that feature dramatic demonstrations of courage, selflessness and sacrifice. The supreme act of agape love, obviously, was Christ's death on the cross for the sins of the entire world. The apostle John tells us "We ought to lay down our lives for our brothers" (v. 16). But then, as if he realized that his readers need practical help with the less dramatic encounters of the every day, John goes on to say that real love involves sharing one's possessions, seeing his brother in need and doing something about it.

In short, says John, "Let us not love with words or tongue but with actions and in truth" (v. 18).

We All Need Deposits in the Love Bank

As someone once said, "Life is so daily." Every time you meet anyone throughout your day, you are talking to a brother or sister in need of encouragement and love.

In *His Needs, Her Needs*,[1] an insightful discussion of how to "affair proof" your marriage, Dr. Willard Harley describes what he calls the "Love Bank"—a mental/emotional recorder deep within all of us that registers positive and negative experiences on a 24-hour-a-day basis.

Dr. Harley's figurative love bank works on a principle of *deposits* and *withdrawals* of a certain amount of *love units*, depending on the kind of encounter you have with the other person. It works like this:

Deposits	Withdrawals
+1—Comfortable encounter	-1—Uncomfortable encounter
+2—Feel good encounter	-1—Feel bad encounter
+3—Feel very good encounter	-3—Feel very bad encounter
+4—Super terrific encounter	-4—Terrible, horrendous encounter

Here is an example of how the love bank functions between two friends: Ann meets her friend, Sally, and Sally's greeting leaves Ann feeling comfortable. Therefore,

THe LoVe BaNK
NeVeR cLoses.
iT is aLways oPeN,
aLways iN Need
oF DeposiTs and
always ReaDY
To DisPeNse
WITHDRAWaLs.

Sally gets a deposit of one unit in Ann's love bank. Ann and Sally have a brief conversation that makes Ann feel especially good (Sally compliments her on her dinner party the other night). This gets Sally a deposit of two units in Ann's love bank.

Ann and Sally are having such a great time together, they decide to go out to lunch. They share with even greater depth and warmth and Ann is feeling very good— so Sally gets a deposit of three more units in Ann's love bank.

A couple of weeks later, Ann and Sally attend the women's retreat sponsored by their church. They have an absolutely outstanding time and Ann and Sally draw much closer as friends and spiritual confidantes. Ann feels that Sally has become the best friend she has ever had and that Sally is very spiritual and perceptive. The entire weekend is one of the highlights of Ann's Christian experience. Sally gets a deposit of four more units in Ann's love bank.

A negative example of the above would reverse the entire process, with Sally saying and doing negative things that would cause withdrawals of love units from Ann's love bank. And, of course, the entire process is functioning from Sally's side, too, with Ann making deposits or withdrawals in Sally's love bank, according to the kind of encounters the two of them may have.

Dr. Harley observes that some people continually build substantial deposits in your love bank. Others may build more modest amounts, and still others may more or less stay even, sometimes making deposits and sometimes making withdrawals. And then there are those people who will go into the red. Your encounters with them will result in far more withdrawals than deposits because they make you feel uncomfortable almost all of the time.

The love bank isn't real, of course, but it is a graphic

way to describe the feelings and attitudes we build as we relate to one another. Obviously, the love bank process is very much at work in a marriage, and Dr. Harley uses many illustrations to show how extramarital affairs can start because withdrawals begin to exceed deposits in one spouse's love bank—or, in some cases, both partners make more withdrawals than deposits.

But the love bank theory is basic to any kind of relationship. Keep in mind that everyone you know on even a casual basis, has an account in your love bank and vice versa. *And, the love bank never closes.* It is always open, always in need of deposits and always ready to dispense withdrawals.

Remember, too, that there are different ways to do "love banking." If you want to run your love bank on an eros or phileo basis, you will expect people to make as many deposits in your love bank as you make in theirs. In other words, you will expect people to give you as many pleasant and comfortable experiences as you give to them. That way you can always stay and get your fair share of loving treatment from everyone else.

But if you run your love bank on an agape basis, you will be far more concerned with making deposits in the love banks of others than in having them making deposits in yours.

And how do we make deposits? Paul gave no better list than the one in 1 Corinthians 13:

> Love is patient, love is kind. It does not envy, it does not boast, it is not proud. It is not rude, it is not self-seeking, it is not easily angered, it keeps no records of wrongs. Love does not delight in evil but rejoices with the truth. It always protects, always trusts, always hopes, always perseveres. Love never fails (vv. 4-8).

What If My Love Bank Becomes Empty?

About now it would be easy to think of a practical problem. It's all well and good to want to make deposits in the love banks of others, but what about *your* love bank? Who makes deposits there? What if you "run out of funds"?

Ideally, in a local body of Christian believers, everybody should constantly seek to make deposits in the love banks of others, always doing it on an unconditional basis, not expecting equal deposits in return. That's good theory, but not much fun to practice on a continual basis if you're

IT IS FROM GOD'S INFINITE LOVE BANK THAT WE GET THE DEPOSITS WE NEED TO KEEP US GOING!

not getting any deposits from other people. Are you going through a time when you don't seem to be getting many love deposits from anyone? Are all your encounters resulting in withdrawals? What now?

Paul certainly knew what that was like. In some of the churches he founded—especially in Corinth—the members made far more withdrawals than deposits in the apostle Paul's love bank. And when he was imprisoned in Rome, he practically became a forgotten man. In another prison Epistle, he writes to Timothy and tells of being deserted by his friends. He is thankful for a believer named Onesiphorus who was not ashamed of Paul's chains and searched diligently throughout Rome until he found him and made some badly needed deposits in the Apostle's love bank! (see 2 Tim. 1:15-17).

How did Paul make it through the dry spells, when his love bank was open for deposits but had no customers? The same way all believers do. The first thing any Christian experiences is God's love. It is from God's infinite love bank that we get the deposits we need to keep us going, even when deposits by our Christian brothers and sisters are slow in coming in. In the meantime, we continue to try to make agape love deposits in the love banks of others on an unconditional basis, with no strings attached, no quid pro quo clause that says, "Well, I love you; now it's your turn to give me something back."

Granted, this isn't easy. Maybe that's why Paul prayed that the love the Philippians had for one another would abound more and more in knowledge and depth of insight (see v. 9).

This knowledge Paul refers to is spiritual—a full and complete knowledge of God through Jesus Christ. The Greek word Paul uses here in Philippians 1:9 is the same one he used in 1 Corinthians 13:12, when he talked about growing up into Christian maturity, putting away childish things and *knowing God fully,* even as God fully knows us.

This kind of knowledge comes only through consistent study of Scripture, and prayer. There are no shortcuts. William Barclay observes that if we love a subject we want to know more and more about it. If we truly love Christ, we want to know more and more about Him and His will for our lives.

Our study of the Bible should be done with sensitivity to Christ and the example He has set. After all, a lot of people didn't make many deposits in His love bank either!

What Agape Love Is Not

The more we value Christ and His presence in our lives, the more our knowledge will be tempered with depth of insight or good judgment. Agape love tries to separate the important from the unimportant, and to see what may do more harm than good. For example, a ridiculous illustration of a poor way to show love would be giving an affectionate bear hug to someone with a dislocated disc. But there are far more subtle ways that we can try to love without good judgment. For example:

. . . Giving someone financial assistance in a way that embarrasses him or reduces his self-esteem to shreds is not agape love.

. . . Setting a wayward friend straight for "her own good" with no regard for her feelings is not agape love.

. . . Coming down on your children with all kinds of authoritarian attitudes because you "want to bring them up in the nurture and admonition of the Lord" is not agape love. It is only a good way to provoke them to wrath (see Eph. 6:4).

The kind of love that causes hurt feelings is not love at all but self-indulgence. Such love doesn't celebrate life, it consumes the feelings of others to feed its own insecurities and collects spiritual scalps to shore up its own sagging ego.

Love that is knowledgeable and insightful will seek to "discern what is best" (Phil. 1:10). The Greek word for discern refers to the testing of metals or coins to see if they are genuine and without alloy. Discerning love can tell the false from the true, the good from the bad, the real from the counterfeit.

Real love, says Paul, is "pure and blameless." The Greek word he uses for "pure" is hard to translate, but it could picture something pure enough to be held up to the light of the sun and reveal no flaws.

By blameless Paul may be suggesting the kind of love that never causes others to stumble. It is possible to be too spiritual—possessed of an uncanny ability to utter the right cliche' or Bible verse at just the wrong time.

It is possible to be so good and so faultless that you drive people away from Christ with nonverbal signals that come across as critical and condemning. How then can we check ourselves and our body language to be sure it bears the fruit of righteousness, not sour grapes or sweet lemons?

In his excellent book, *Speaking from the Heart*, Ken Durham says Christian body language isn't based on certain pious phrases or expressions. Real Christian body language "is not measured in the quantity of religious words, but in the Christlike quality of both our words and lives that give credibility to our words."[2] As Paul put it so well, the Christian's love is "filled with the fruit of righteousness that comes through Jesus Christ—to the glory and praise of God" (Phil. 1:11).

Don't Miss the Sunset

Paul has packed a tremendous truth into his one sentence prayer here at the beginning of his letter to the church at Philippi. Paul knows that love is what makes life enjoyable—lovely and beautiful. He wants the Philippians—and us—to not shove love into the background while we try to dot all the *I*'s and cross all the *T*'s in our "To Do List."

Life has a way of becoming too busy. The important can easily give way to the urgent, which demands efficiency and speed. Paul valued faith, hope and love but he was careful to add that the greatest of these was love (see 1 Cor. 13:13). He knew that ever so subtly (or not so subtly), we can become consumers and collectors rather than celebrators of God's love in Christ.

We can be like the art students who went on a field trip to a spot where the sunset was particularly spectacular. As the sunset blazed across the hill in lovely pinks, reds, oranges and yellows, the teacher urged his class to paint as fast as possible to catch all of the beauty they could. As he walked among his students, he noticed one young man who was very busy painting the shingles of the barn at the foot of the hill. There before him a gorgeous sunset lit the entire sky, but on his canvas all he had were the shingles of a barn.

"Forget the shingles!" cried the teacher. "They're just details. Paint the sunset!"

We dare not miss the point of this simple parable. The urgent details and so-called essential things of life are the shingles. The sunset is Christ's love. If we don't paint life with His love, we may look up to learn we have spent a lot of time being very good at details and "To Do Lists" and have missed the greatest thing of all.

But where do we begin? We value love, but what about all the goofs we have made, as recently as last night or this morning? Instead of wallowing in guilt, we can start somewhere and take even the smallest step toward enjoying more and more of Christ's love, forgiveness and power.

Do some love banking with Jesus each day and then go out to make investments based on His knowledge and depth of insight. There are all kinds of love banks out there waiting to be filled with your deposits.

You can't miss them—if you are willing to look!

The following questions are designed for your personal study or to discuss with a group. Record your answers in your journal/notebook.

1. Do you agree or disagree with the observation: "Every time you meet anyone throughout your day, you are talking to a brother or sister in need of encouragement, strokes and love." If you agree, how should this affect your attitude and actions? Be specific.

2. What is the basic difference between *agape* love and

eros or *phileo* love? What kind of love does Scripture command the Christian to demonstrate?

3. What does *agape* love look or feel like? (see John 3:16; 1 John 3:16-18).

4. According to Dr. Willard Harley's "Love Bank" theory, how do people make deposits and withdrawals in each other's love bank? What happens when someone builds up a large account in someone else's love bank? What happens when someone goes in the red? What does this suggest about how Christians should treat one another?

5. What can you do if you hit a "dry spell" and get few or no deposits in your love bank from others—even other Christians? Does Paul's prayer in Philippians 1:9-11 give any useful suggestions?

6. Why does Paul link knowledge and depth of insight with love in verse 9? Compare 1 Corinthians 13:12. How can we know God more fully?

7. This chapter lists some examples of what *agape* love *is not*. Can you think of others? Why is it so important to have discernment and insight when trying to love others? What if you have to do something that will inevitably hurt someone's feelings? (Examples: confront a friend about gossiping or other inappropriate behavior; discipline your children.)

8. How can you gain the discernment and insight you need to live life effectively and fruitfully? Compare Philippians 1:11 with John 15:1-6; Galatians 5:22-26; James 3:17.

Taking Stock and Setting Goals

1. I practice *agape* love best when:

2. I practice *agape* love least when:

3. People who need a deposit from me in their love banks are (list specific names):

4. I will seek to make these love deposits by (list specific actions):

Lord, make me more perceptive

"Help me remember that everyone I meet each day needs a stroke, a word of encouragement—a deposit in his or her love bank. Please keep making your deposits in my love bank so I can know the difference between what is important and what is not, and be able to discern what will do more harm than good. Empower me to always do more good than harm.

Notes
1. Willard F. Harley, Jr., *His Needs, Her Needs* (Old Tappan, NJ: Fleming H. Revell Co., 1986).
2. Ken Durham, *Speaking from the Heart* (Fort Worth, TX: Sweet Publishing Co., 1986), p. 33.

CHAPTER THREE

How much do you value commitment? Before answering, it might help to take this little quiz. Do you agree or disagree with the following statements?

> Commitment is basic to any kind of substantial relationship.
>
> Commitment equals dependability.
>
> We make commitments only for the good of others or for a good cause.
>
> Many people claim to be Christians, but they don't act that committed.
>
> Commitment to the local church and its ministry has been eroded by materialism and other worldly influences.

There are no right answers to the above quiz, but most people have rather firm opinions. Many would agree that commitment is basic to any kind of substantial relationship. How can you have a relationship if you aren't committed to one another? they ask. On the other hand, people enter into substantial relationships all the time like marriage and business contracts, but aren't really committed. They may have a legal or technical commitment to meet, but their hearts are somewhere else.

It seems logical enough to say that commitment would equal dependability. But if I fail on one or two occasions to be dependable, does that mean I am uncommitted?

You may agree that commitments are made only for the good of others or for a good cause. At least, they should be made on this basis. But we often make commitments for our own good, for what we can get out of it. We may not want to admit this, but it certainly happens.

Commitment Is a Relative Term

Talking about the commitments of Christians and how shallow or deep they are is always provocative. Sometimes this depends on where you go to church, or the type of Christians you spend time with. One Christian's commitment can be another Christian's apathy.

Jon Johnston, in *Will Evangelicalism Survive Its Own Popularity?*, believes that too many Christians suffer from a modern day brand of *pleonexia,* what the Greeks called "an accursed love of having." He writes: "Our first allegiance is to mammon rather than God . . . the first fruits of our life's energies and priorities are directed toward the desire to accumulate."[1]

Edward Dayton, vice president for Mission and Evangelism of World Vision International, believes: "Although the number of Christians multiplies, the depth of their Christianity seems shallow." He observes that while Christians have an overabundance of how-to books on everything from sex and marriage to being better Bible students, "fewer and fewer of us feel at peace."[2]

When I asked a friend about his Christian commitment, he said, "To my small group and personal relationship to

Christ, I'm strong," he said. "To my church, I'm so-so."

His attitude is not unusual. Many people join churches and have their own idea of just how committed they will be. "They won't necessarily miss me at church this Sunday," they tell themselves. "Besides, I've earned a rest." How ironic that some church members consider a day off from Sunday services as a rest, but that is often the term they use in describing their weekend out of town or at the beach.

Paul's Approach to Commitment

What kind of book would Paul write about Christians and their commitment today? It's hard to say, but we do know what he wrote to Christians some 19 centuries ago. In the first chapter of Philippians, Paul rejoices because his circumstances have turned out for the good even though he is in prison. The cause of Christ is even becoming well-known throughout Caesar's crack praetorian guard, his hand-picked soldiers who have been assigned to guard Paul all day long by being chained to him. Naturally, Paul wouldn't miss this kind of opportunity, and more than one Roman soldier became a captive audience and later a convert because of his exposure to Paul's convincing witness.

But even more indicative of Paul's commitment to Jesus is his reaction to getting news about some Christians who are trying to take advantage of his imprisonment by increasing their own popularity in ministries. Paul doesn't care. Even if some people preach the gospel out of envy and strife to forward their own selfish ambitions, it's all right with him. "What does it matter?" asks Paul. "The important thing is that in every way, whether from false motives or true, Christ is preached. And because of this I rejoice" (Phil. 1:18).

Paul's only worry is that he might do something that would cause him to feel ashamed because he wasn't bold enough to speak for Christ when he should. He hopes that he can always "be an honor to Christ, whether I live or whether I must die. For to me, living means opportunities for Christ, and dying—well, that's better yet!" (vv. 20,21, *TLB*).

The choice left him in a total dilemma. He was torn between the two. He desired to depart and be with Christ, but he saw the necessity to remain a minister in Christ's name as long as he could.

When Paul talks about departing, he uses the word that describes the striking of camp, taking down the tents and moving on. Paul sounds as if he would like to strike his own earthly tent, but he cannot. He knows he must remain and continue with the Philippians and all other believers for their progress and joy in the faith. Paul's commitment to Christ committed him completely to other members of the Body, which is something to think about the next time we want to head for the beach to get a rest from attending Sunday services.

Down through the centuries, many giants of the Christian faith have tried to match Paul's level of commitment. The story of one such man made an Academy Award-winning film.

His Chariot Took Him to China

Eric Liddle's commitment to athletic excellence was well documented in the film *Chariots of Fire*. But his commitment to his Christian values was what made headlines when he refused to compete in the 100-meter dash during the 1924 Olympic games because the race was scheduled for a Sunday. Nonetheless, Liddle went on to set a world record in the 400-meter dash and win a Gold Medal. If you saw the film, you may recall the sobering note that appeared on the screen as the final credits rolled.

> Eric Liddle, missionary
> Died in occupied China
> At the end of World War II
> All of Scotland mourned.

Following the '24 games, Liddle could have basked in fame and glory in his native Britain, but in less than a year he left for China to serve with the London Missionary Society, just as his father had done. For part of Liddle's 21-year career in China, he taught science courses at the Anglo-Chinese College in Tientsin. Later, he did evangelism work in rural areas, usually traveling over rough terrain on foot or bicycle.

One example of Eric Liddle's courage and commitment came out of his rescue of two wounded men during a war between China and Japan in the late 1930s. He heard of the first man, who lay dying in a bombed out temple back in the hills. No local Chinese villagers would help, fearing the wrath of occupying Japanese soldiers. Liddle feared for his life as well, but he persuaded a Chinese workman to help, and they set out with a crude cart to try to rescue the wounded man.

It was a two-day journey, but they finally found the poor fellow and loaded him into the cart. On their perilous trek back to the mission hospital they discovered a second badly wounded resistance fighter, who had been left for dead after being slashed by a Japanese officer's sword.

Though it meant taking even greater risks, Eric Liddle and his companion picked up the other wounded man and, because there was no room left in the cart, had to place him on the shafts of the crude vehicle. They hauled its heavy load 18 more miles to a nearby hospital where both men survived and the one with the sword slash in the neck became a follower of Jesus Christ.

The Chinese/Japanese struggle continued into the early 1940s and a few weeks before the bombing of Pearl Harbor, Liddle was imprisoned by the Japanese, just after getting his wife and two children out of China.

Liddle hoped he would be able to join his family, but the months in captivity stretched into years as he lived among 1800 people crammed into a compound only 150 x 200 yards. Seldom mentioning his Olympic career or his Gold Medal, he preferred to help by teaching and tutoring and giving special care to the older people who were weak and ill. He continually helped organize and run Christian meetings that became a critical part of keeping many people alive in the squalor of open cesspools, rats, flies and disease.

Just a few months before the camp was liberated, a brain tumor took Eric Liddle's life, but he let few know of his tremendous pain and suffering. To the last day he continued moving about, walking slowly under trees near the camp hospital where he taught the children games. His smile never faded, but he died the next evening. He was buried in a little cemetery in the camp with an honor guard made up of the children who had meant so much to him while being separated from his own family.

One of those children was David Mitchell, who later wrote: "None of us will ever forget this man who was totally committed to putting God first, a man whose humble life combined muscular Christianity with radiant godliness. What was his secret? He unreservedly committed his life to Jesus Christ as his Savior and Lord. That friendship meant everything to him. In the cramped men's dormitory, early each morning by the flickering oil of a peanut oil lamp, he and a roommate studied the Bible and talked with God for an hour. As a Christian, Eric Liddle's desire was to know God more deeply, and, as a missionary, to make Him known more fully."[3]

For Eric Liddle, Paul's words have special meaning. For him to live was Christ, and to die was gain.

Sticking Around for the Long Haul

Eric Liddle valued commitment because he valued Jesus Christ above all else in life. According to the dictionary, a *commitment* is "a pledge to do something". It means that you are bound emotionally or intellectually to a specific course of action or belief.

Commitment equals "sticking around for the long haul." Perhaps few can equal the record set by "Aunt Effie" Linquist who, for over 80 years, faithfully attended the First Baptist Church of Keokuk, Iowa, until a broken hip kept her confined at home.

At the age of 93 Aunt Effie was honored by the church with a special reception that recognized her attendance at 80 consecutive Christmas, New Year's and Easter services, as well as 960 monthly communion Sundays. During that time, she was "at the church pretty near every time the door was open."

In her lifetime, Aunt Effie listened to over 8,000 sermons and attended more than 4,000 prayer meetings, under the ministry of 15 different pastors, many of whom considered her a personal confidante. She taught Sunday School for over 50 years, with an intense love for her pupils that always set her apart from other teachers. On March 8, 1980, at age 97, Effie Linquist's commitment was rewarded when she met Jesus face to face.[4]

ONE OF THE GREATEST HELPS IN FULFILLING ANY COMMITMENT IS TO TELL YOUR FRIENDS ABOUT WHAT YOU'RE TRYING TO DO. ONCE YOU'VE ANNOUNCED YOUR INTENTIONS, IT'S HARD TO TURN BACK.

Increasing Your Commitment Quotient

In his book, *Reaching Your Possibilities Through Commitment,* Gerald W. Marshall, lists four basic steps that are always involved in becoming committed. Marshall's "Four C's of Commitment" include:

1. *Choose* your commitments carefully, rather than on the spur of the moment or without thinking it through.

2. *Commit* yourself firmly and specifically. Identify target dates and the particular actions you need to consistently perform in order to carry out your commitment.

3. *Coordinate* all of your resources in order to be able to hit your commitment target.

4. Never quit until you *complete* your commitment (unless what you are doing has become harmful or destructive to you and others).

Marshall believes that one of the greatest helps in fulfilling any commitment is to tell your friends and acquaintances about what you're trying to do. Once you've announced your intentions, it's hard to turn back. Furthermore, your friends can encourage you and pray for your success.

A 45-year-old amateur at long distance running, Marshall tried his four C's system by committing himself to run in a marathon in Dallas, Texas. Never having run 26 miles before, he made his commitment specific by openly telling friends and associates what he planned to do. Then he marshaled all of his resources by training hard and eating right. On the day of the marathon, he showed up ready to make the supreme effort.

For the first 17 and a half miles, Marshall surprised himself, but then he stopped to change shoes and rest a bit. That was a mistake. First, a fellow runner who had also stopped nearby, groaned that he was quitting. He had hit that famous "wall" all marathoners experience somewhere between 15 and 20 miles. Marshall began wondering if maybe he shouldn't quit, too, and when he tried to stand up, the thought became even more appealing because he had cooled down, gotten stiff and could barely move!

The only thing that got Marshall out on the road again was realizing that he had told many of his friends about his commitment and that he knew some of them would be praying for him. He couldn't walk in on Monday and admit he had failed. Somehow he covered the last eight and a half miles, alternately walking and running. Earlier finishers and spectators were still there to cheer him on as he "sprinted" across the finish line with his last ounce of energy.

At 4 hours, 39 minutes and 58 seconds, Marshall had set no marathon records, but he didn't care. He had *finished,* exactly what he had committed himself to do. He was physically spent, but psychologically and spiritually exhilarated.

Commenting on what it all meant, he said, "It showed me how great God was when He created man and what wonderful strength He gave to us. It showed me that God had made me to excel and grow. I had tasted of just a part of my inherent potential and it was fantastic. I was filled with wonder, joy, and reverence as I realized I had experienced Isaiah 40:31: 'But those who hope in the Lord will

COMMITMENT keeps US GOING.

renew their strength. They will soar on wings like eagles; they will run and not grow weary, they will walk and not be faint.'"[5]

What Happens If You Get Tired?

Gerald Marshall's marathon experience is a picture of the Christian life. We make a commitment to follow Christ and we start out on a race that will last for life. Along the way we get tired so we sit down to rest a little. We hear others say they are quitting and we think perhaps we should, too. Or we stiffen up and don't think we can get moving again.

But somehow commitment keeps us going.

It is doubtful Paul wrote the letter to the Hebrews, but these words from chapter 12 sound a great deal like him: "Therefore, since we are surrounded by such a great cloud of witnesses, let us throw off everything that hinders and the sin that so easily entangles, and let us run with perseverance the race marked out for us. Let us fix our eyes on Jesus, the author and perfecter of our faith, who for the joy set before him endured the cross, scorning its shame, and sat down at the right hand of the throne of God" (Heb. 12:1,2). A key to running the Christian race with perseverance is to fix your eyes on Jesus, and none other.

Because he is a graduate of Texas A&M, Gerald Marshall has been the brunt of a lot of "Texas Aggie" jokes over the years. One of his favorites is about the Aggie who bought a new, heavy-duty chain saw that was guaranteed to cut three cords of firewood a day. After several days of hard labor with the saw, he brought it back to the dealer. He complained that it would only cut one cord a day and asked to have it checked out. The dealer took it and pulled the start rope to test it out and it started immediately. Suddenly the Aggie got wide-eyed, jumped back and said, "Where is all that noise coming from?"[6]

Marshall observes that we often try to live our Christian lives the same way the Aggie tried to use his chain saw. Instead of turning on the power and letting the Spirit of God work in us, we try to do all the work and carry the burden ourselves. But, "if we will turn Him on in our lives and let Him work through us, we can do amazing things."[7]

Or, in the words of the Apostle who believed living was Christ and dying was gain: "I can do everything God asks me to with the help of Christ who gives me the strength and power" (Phil. 4:13, *TLB*).

A KEY TO RUNNING THE CHRISTIAN RACE WITH PERSEVERANCE IS TO FIX YOUR EYES ON JESUS, AND NONE OTHER.

The following questions are designed for your personal study or to discuss with a group. Record your answers in your journal/notebook.

1. What were your answers to the agree/disagree statements at the opening of the chapter? Which statement aroused the most feeling or strongest opinion? What does this tell you about your values?

2. Reread the statements by Jon Johnston and Edward Dayton. Do you think they are judging Christians too harshly? How do their statements apply to you?

3. Reread the statement by the friend who said his commitment to his small group and relationship to Christ was strong but his commitment to church was "so-so." On a scale of 1 to 10, with 10 being high, what is your commitment to your church? How does it compare to your commitment to Christ? Why is it easy to rationalize, "They won't necessarily miss me at church this Sunday—besides, I've earned a rest"?

4. Why is Paul such an outstanding example of Christian commitment? (see Phil. 1:12-25).

5. Why did Paul want to depart and be with Christ? What kept him here?

6. What did Eric Liddle do following the Olympic Games of 1924 to demonstrate his commitment to Christ?

Could he have chosen another path and been just as committed? In what sense? Reread the story of Eric Liddle's imprisonment by the Japanese during World War II. Which of his actions is most significant to you in regard to indicating his commitment?

7. How would you define the word *commitment*? How does it compare to the definition in this chapter?

8. How can commitment keep you going even when you get tired? What forces are at work?

9. The story of the Texas Aggie and the chain saw points up the need to "turn on the power" and not do all the work yourself. List some ways to turn on the Holy Spirit's power in your own life and let Him work through you.

Taking Stock and Setting Goals

1. On a scale of 1 to 10, with 10 being high, my commitment to Christ is _____ .

2. On a scale of 1 to 10, with 10 being high, my commitment to my church is _____ .

3. Reread Gerald Marshall's "Four C's of Commitment." Which of these do you use regularly? Which do you need to use more often? How do you plan to do this?

Lord, I want to be committed

Build into the fibers of my being the kind of dependability

that makes me someone to be counted on—in the middle of the night by a friend in need, or on Sunday morning by my church, which needs me also. Keep me aware, Lord, that I am not a Lone Ranger Christian—that I am called into a community of believers and it is there that my commitment is proven or found wanting.

Notes

1. Jon Johnston, *Will Evangelicalism Survive Its Own Popularity?* (Grand Rapids, MI: Zondervan Publishing House, 1980), p. 90.
2. Edward R. Dayton, *Whatever Happened to Commitment?* (Grand Rapids, MI: Zondervan Publishing House, 1983), p. 19.
3. Eric H. Liddle, *Disciplines of the Christian Life* (Nashville, TN: Abingdon Press, 1985), see "I Remember Eric Liddle" by David J. Mitchell, pp. 12-18.
4. Paul Lee Tan, *Encyclopedia of 7700 Illustrations* (Garland, TX: Assurance Publishers, 1979), p. 242.
5. Gerald W. Marshall, *Reaching Your Possibilities Through Commitment* (Ventura, CA: Regal Books, 1981), pp. 75,76.
6. Ibid., p. 77.
7. Ibid., pp. 77,78.

CHAPTER FOUR
THE SECRET OF A WINNING TEAM

You may have heard it said, "We become Christians one at a time, but we are to live Christianity together." Unity is another value with special meaning to followers of Christ. Jesus spent a lot of time trying to get His disciples to practice more and better unity, and Paul spoke of it often in his letters to the churches he planted across the world. Why does Scripture speak so often of unity, or what could also be called *teamwork*?

Part of the answer lies in the dangers of individualism. One of the most insidious enemies of unity in the church today is the self-centeredness that encourages dissension, conceit, pride, factions and lack of teamwork. While most Christians are appalled by the philosophy that advises "Look out for Number One," many still practice individualism at church by keeping other members at arm's length. Individualism means being content to arrive for services, "Get what I can out of the message," shake a few hands, tell people "I'm fine," and leave, not to appear until the next Sunday.

In *Defeating the Dragons of the World*, Stephen Eyre observes that there are a few churches where people drink deeply from each other but, sad to say, these churches are few and far between. There are just too many churches where intimacy is a stranger and the dragon of individualism reigns supreme. According to Eyre, the dragon's creed is, "I am the source of my own value." He manages to keep people locked inside themselves while locking others out.[1]

Part of this is our American tradition and heritage. We are rugged individuals in the style of John Wayne or Lee Iacocca. But like most good things, rugged individualism has gone to seed and created self-centered navel gazers who are more preoccupied with themselves than anything else. We say we value Christ and fellowship with other believers, but we value our independence and freedom more. Restraint, self-discipline and commitment are not favorite words. After all, "I gotta be me!"

The result is an inhibiting of the unity and teamwork that is so badly needed to create effective ministry. Many people want the church to minister to them, but they seem to have no clue about having the responsibility to become a functioning part of the Body that ministers to itself, as its members minister to one another. When we lack the humility to open up to each other and care about each other, we can become caterpillars, wrapped up in our cocoon of Number One, unaware of how to break out and become butterflies who can fulfill an unlimited number of opportunities for Christ.

Perhaps that's why Paul stresses values like unity and teamwork so much. As mature as the Philippian church apparently was, its members were still human and had their problems, including individualism, which threatened their unity.

Are the Philippians committed? Are they determined to conduct themselves in a manner worthy of the gospel of Christ? Paul opens chapter two of his letter with a brief "if-then" argument: *If* being united to Christ is encouraging; *if* his love is comforting; *if* the Holy Spirit is working in your life at all producing any kind of tenderness or compassion; *if* . . . *then*, says Paul, you can "make my joy complete by being like-minded, having the same love, being one in spirit and purpose" (Phil. 2:1,2).

HUMILITY IS SOMETHING WE ALL DESIRE BUT WE AREN'T QUITE SURE WHAT IT IS.

I AM HUMBLE

In Philippians 2:3,4, Paul lists three big reasons why we don't work together as well as we could. The church suffers from discord and disunity because people are ambitious, proud and self-centered. Paul says Christians should "do nothing out of selfish ambition or vain conceit, but in humility, consider others better" than themselves. Each Christian should look not only to his or her own interests, but also to the interests of others (see vv. 3,4).

Sin Is the Flip Side of Virtue

It's ironic that so many sins are the flip side of so many virtues. There is nothing wrong with ambition. Without ambition, we become sluggards, and Solomon had some choice words to say about that (see Prov. 6:6-9, 26:15,16). With too much ambition, however, we become greedy and selfish, wanting to advance ourselves, and not the work of Christ (see 1 Tim. 6:10; Jas. 5:3).

Talk to any coach of the sport that demands teamwork (basketball or football, for example), and he can tell you about outstanding athletes he has benched or cut because they weren't team players. They were more interested in running up individual statistics for themselves than helping the team win.

Selfish Ambition usually has a twin brother called Vain Conceit—that consuming desire to make a good impression, and to gain the ooh's and aah's of onlookers. The selfish athlete who tries to do it all himself is called a glory hog for good reason. He is in it for one thing—the thrill of *personal* glory. For many people, personal prestige is much more important than money. They value being known, admired, respected and called on to give their opinion. They like being famous, even if it's as a big fish in a small pond.

If Selfish Ambition and Vain Conceit are twins, Self-centeredness is their first cousin. Concentrate on yourself and you inevitably put down, ignore and neglect others.

Seventeenth-century poet, John Donne, penned the familiar line, "No man is an island, entire of itself." Paul anticipated Donne by 16 centuries or so when he observed that there are no islands in the Body of Christ. When he wrote to the Corinthians, who were as infested with individualism as any group could be, Paul said: "The body is a unit, though it is made up of many parts . . . for we were all baptized by one Spirit into one body . . . now you are the body of Christ, and each one of you is a part of it" (1 Cor. 12:12,13,27).

Body Parts Should Work Together

Business executive and management training specialist, John Noe, believes the powerful synergy God has built into our human bodies can become just as evident in human relationships, if people learn to work together the way our body parts do. Noe recalls when he trained for two years by running the back roads of Indiana to prepare himself to scale the world's most classic mountain, the 14,780-foot Matterhorn of Switzerland. Compared to Everest or Kilimanjaro, which tower almost 30,000 feet, the Matterhorn doesn't sound that high, but its jagged overhang, icy slopes and bone-chilling winds have killed many climbers.

As John Noe ran and did other exercises to prepare himself for the climb, he kept looking down at his feet and saying, "One day these feet are going to stand on top of the Matterhorn!" When he finally made that awesome climb to the summit, he was constantly aware of how his body worked as a unit: His feet searched for solid foot holes as his hands grasped at crevices and edges of sharp rock; his legs strained with his arms to lift his weight ever higher, as his lungs and heart pumped overtime to convert the thin air into oxygen and send the blood racing through his veins to keep him from freezing to death in the vicious cold.

Noe made it to the top, and one of the photographs that means the most to him shows only his feet standing on the rocky pinnacle of the Matterhorn. That picture has special meaning, says Noe, "Only because my feet were attached to me."[2]

In John Noe's illustration of what body parts can do together to scale a mountain, we find a tremendous truth for the Body of Christ and its many members. When Christians fail to work together and go off in opposite directions, some to scale mountains that they alone have chosen to climb while leaving others behind or uninvited, the Body of Christ is not helped nor hindered. Individual Christians may gain prominence and prestige but the Body suffers. As Noe puts it, "None of us can truly say, 'I am' until he or she can truly say, 'We are!'"[3]

Humility Is Hard to Define

Paul's answer to Selfish Ambition, Vain Conceit and Self-centeredness is simple: "In humility consider others better than yourselves. Each of you should look not only to your own interests, but also to the interests of others" (Phil. 2:3,4). Humility is something we all desire but we aren't quite sure what it is. Some confuse self-negation (putting oneself down) with humility. Others believe it is in the total eradication of self, a kind of neurotic humility that says, "I am so bad or hopeless, even God can't do much for me." At its extreme, neurotic humility can turn into self-hatred, feeling absolutely no self-worth whatsoever.

In Christian circles, it is popular to practice humility by using the timeworn phrase, "I didn't do it; the Lord did." Some people will modestly say this when congratulated for how well they sing, teach or even hit a backhand in tennis. It is strange, however, that the Lord seldom gets credit for a high note that goes flat, a lesson that turns sour or a backhand that sails into the net.

The fact is, God does empower us as we ask Him to and as we walk in the Spirit. But God does not turn a monotone voice into a lovely soprano, nor do you develop a great backhand by watching Wimbledon on TV. God does nothing for us that He hasn't equipped us to do for ourselves through hard work and long hours of practice and effort. That's what it means to work out your own salvation while God works within you to give you the will and the energy (see v. 12).

While the meaning of humility is hard to pin down, we get some clues if we go back to the root Latin word for humility, *humus*, which means "ground." The humble man is one who lives, so to speak, on the ground floor. The humble man does not lift himself up and try to put himself above others. It helps to remember that Satan was once Lucifer, one of God's angels who was star of the morning until he tried to lift himself up, literally shove God off His throne and become like the Most High (see Isa. 14:12-14).

Lincoln, Schweitzer and Humility

It is easier to illustrate humility than to describe it. Stories involving two of history's most famous men—Abraham Lincoln and Albert Schweitzer—give us hints of what humility is all about.

As the Civil War raged on and men died by the thousands, Lincoln and Secretary of War Edwin Stanton visited the battlefield quarters of General George McClellan. They waited patiently for McClellan to return from the front, but when he finally arrived he gave them no greeting. He simply walked past them and on up the stairs.

Lincoln and Stanton assumed he would be back soon, and continued to wait. After considerable time General McClellan did not appear, so they sent the maid to inquire. She returned and said, "I'm sorry, Mr. President, but the General asked me to tell you that he is tired and has gone to bed."

Secretary of War Stanton was shocked and incensed: "Mr. President, that's unacceptable. You must relieve him of his command."

Lincoln thought about that for a minute and then said, "No, I will not relieve him; that man wins battles. I would hold his horse and wash the dirt from his boots if he could shorten this bloodshed by one hour."[4]

Albert Schweitzer, who gained fame in the field of music, became a medical doctor in later life and lost himself in the African jungles where he devoted his skills to service and saving lives. One day Schweitzer asked one of the Africans who was helping him at the hospital to carry in some wood. The African, who had been learning to read and write, replied, "I'd like to, Sir, but it's beneath my dignity. I am a scholar and intellectual."

Schweitzer chuckled and said, "I've always wanted to be an intellectual, too, but I never quite made it. I'll carry the wood!" Then he went out and did just that.[5]

Paul Goes Right to the Source

These glimpses from the lives of Lincoln and Schweitzer are valuable sketches of humility, but Paul paints a much

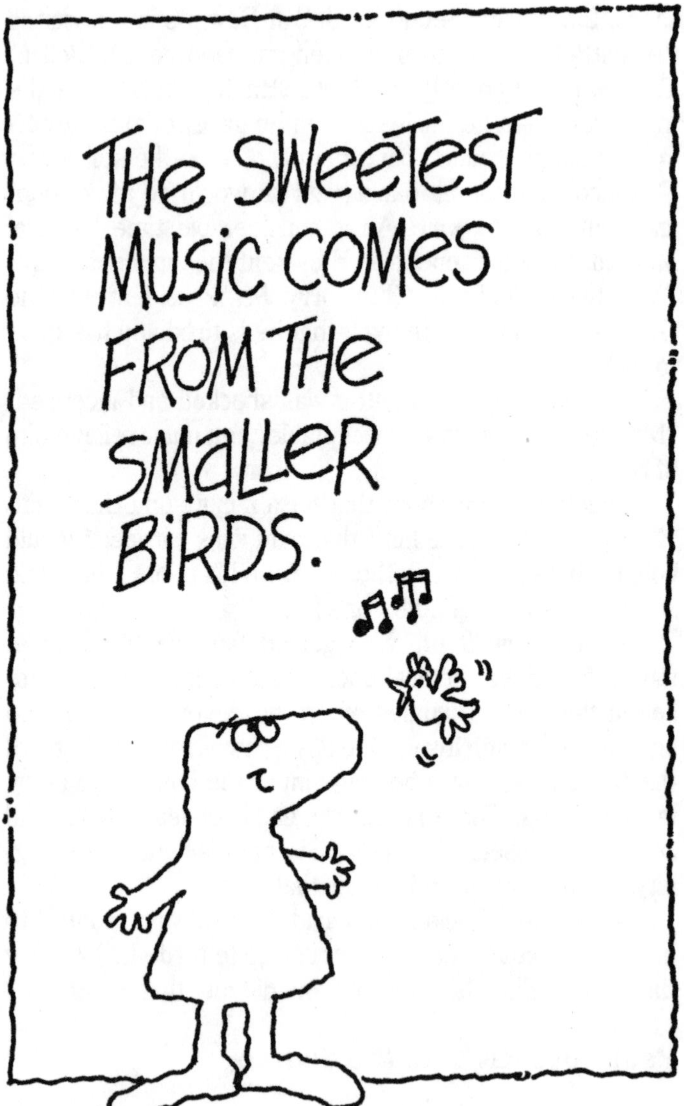
THE SWEETEST MUSIC COMES FROM THE SMALLER BIRDS.

clearer portrait in Philippians 2:5-11: "Your attitude should be the same as that of Christ Jesus: Who, being in very nature God, did not consider equality with God something to be grasped, but made himself nothing, taking the very nature of a servant, being made in human likeness. And being found in appearance as a man, he humbled himself and became obedient to death—even death on a cross!" (Phil. 2:5-8).

Theologians have written volumes about this passage but still haven't fully explained it. Jesus Christ, an equal partner in the Godhead, gave up His rights to riches, glory and authority, to become as fully human as He was fully divine. Why? He came to be a servant and our Savior. As a true servant, He did not assert His rights, He waived them.

Jesus didn't just talk about humility; He modeled it. On the night of the Last Supper, Jesus girded Himself with a towel and taught His disciples a graphic lesson in humility by washing their feet, becoming their servant in a way they could not mistake (see John 13:1-9). Later, after He and His disciples broke bread and drank from the cup to institute the new covenant in His blood, an argument broke out among the disciples about which of them was to be greatest.

Jesus taught them another lesson in humility saying, "The kings of the Gentiles lord it over them; and those who exercise authority over them call themselves Benefactors. But you are not to be like that. Instead, the greatest among you should be like the youngest, and the one who rules like the one who serves. For who is greater, the one who is at the table or the one who serves? Is it not the one who is at the table? But I am among you as one who serves" (Luke 22:25-27).

Again and again Jesus tried to teach His disciples the

YOU CAN'T BE PROUD AND LEAN
ON EACH OTHER AT THE SAME TIME.

wisdom that someone caught in the old epigram: "It is possible to be too big for God to use you, but never too small for God to use you."

In Unity There Is Always Humility

Christian values like unity and humility build on one another like bricks on a wall. John Noe believes the unity principle gets results because it forces us to put aside pride or being status conscious and walk arm in arm instead. He recalls growing up in southern Indiana and how he and his boyhood friends would walk down the railroad tracks on hot summer days. There were three ways to walk the tracks: on the ties, between the ties or on the rails. Walking on the rails provided much smoother footing, but required excellent balance and nobody got very far alone. But John and his buddies worked out a plan that enabled them to walk the rails for a mile or more without falling off.

John would stand on one rail and his friend would be on the other. Then they both leaned over, grasped each other firmly by the arm, and off they would go down the tracks, joined together in perfect teamwork, not missing a step.[6] The lesson is obvious: You can't be proud and lean on each other at the same time.

What Paul is teaching the Philippians and us is that unity and humility always go hand in hand. Unity is always gained at the expense of pride as you work for the good of others and they do the same for you.

Someone has said the sweetest music comes only from the smaller birds. As a matter of fact, only the smaller birds are the ones who really sing. You don't hear many beautiful notes from the turkey, ostrich or the eagle. But you do hear beautiful music from the canary, the wren and the lark. If we want to make beautiful music that is sweet to the Lord's ears, we must become small in our own eyes as we join our voices together to glorify God.

The following questions are designed for your personal study or to discuss with a group. Record your answers in your journal/notebook.

1. Do you agree or disagree with the idea that "We become Christians one at a time but we are to live Christianity together"? Compare Philippians 2:1,2 with Matthew 18:19; Mark 2:3; John 10:16, 17:21; Ephesians 2:14. See also Phillipians 1:27. What is Paul saying here about the need for unity and cooperation?

2. What is individualism and why is it such a powerful enemy of the Body of Christ? Do you believe Christians are aware of how destructive individualism really is? Why or why not?

3. What is the danger in claiming, "I am the source of my own value"? What does the Bible say about the source of the Christian's value? (see Job 32:8; Ps. 8:3-8; Acts 17:26-28).

4. Do you agree or disagree with the statement: "When we lack the humility to open up to each other and care about each other, we can become caterpillars, wrapped in our own cocoon of Number One, unaware of how to break out and become butterflies to fulfill an unlimited number of opportunities for Christ." Did Paul think some of the Philippian Christians were becoming caterpillars? (see Phil. 2:1-4).

5. According to Philippians 2:3,4, what are three big reasons why Christians don't work together as well as they could? Why can a virtue have a flip side that is sin? For example, what can happen if you are too ambitious?

6. How did Jesus model humility? See especially John 13:1-9 and Philippians 2:5-11. Which of His actions or

statements impresses you the most and why?

7. What do the following three statements have in common?

   a. "None of us can truly say, 'I am' until he or she can truly say, 'We are!'"

   b. "No man is an island, entire of itself."

   c. "Now you are the body of Christ, and each one of you is a part of it" (1 Cor. 12:27).

8. Have you ever used the well-known cliché, "I didn't do it; the Lord did"? What were the circumstances? Suppose you sincerely pray for God's guidance and seek to glorify God in doing something but it turns out to be a horrible mistake or a terrible failure. Would you still tell someone, "I didn't do it, the Lord did"? Why or why not?

9. Why is self-negation false humility? How could constantly putting yourself down be a form of pride or self-centeredness?

10. How are the stories about Abraham Lincoln and Albert Schweitzer examples of living out Paul's advice in Philippians 2:3,4?

Taking Stock and Setting Goals

1. For me, individualism is (a) no problem, (b) sometimes a problem, (c) a real problem.

2. On a scale of 1 to 10, with 10 being high, my attempts to build unity in the Body of Christ are:

3. I am humble (a) all of the time, (b) most of the time, (c) some of the time, (d) seldom.

4. Ways I can be aware of the interests of others in my family are:

5. Ways I can put others ahead of myself at church, at work or at home are:

Lord, make me humble

I want to be humble enough to give up selfish ambitions, stubborn opinions or vain conceits in order to have unity and teamwork in the Body. Make me interested in others (as you know, I'm already interested in myself). Lord, I want to have your attitude, but I'm afraid. Your attitude took you to Golgotha and I'm not ready for that. Make me ready.

Notes
1. Stephen D. Eyre, *Defeating the Dragons of the World* (Downers Grove, IL: InterVarsity Press, 1986), p. 62.
2. John R. Noe, *People Power* (Nashville, TN: Oliver-Nelson, Div. of Thomas Nelson Pubs., 1986), pp. 22,23.
3. Ibid., p. 23.
4. Robert A. Schuller, Editor, *Robert H. Schuller Tells You How to Be an Extraordinary Person in an Ordinary World* (Old Tappan, NJ: Fleming H. Revell Co., 1985), pp. 97,98.
5. Ibid., p. 110.
6. Noe, *People Power*, p. 59.

CHAPTER FIVE

HOW TO LIVE FROM THE INSIDE OUT

Any of Paul's letters could be called a spiritual gold mine, but Philippians is an especially rich mother lode of Christian values. Nestled in the middle of chapter 2 is one of the largest nuggets of them all—that old-fashioned virtue/value called *integrity*, something that has all but disappeared from the secular scene and is even an endangered species within the Church.

To get a faint glimpse of how bad things have gotten in the schools, picture the following scene enacted in a New Jersey classroom. The teacher poses this situation to her 15 pupils: A woman finds $1,000 lying on the street, picks it up and turns it in. Did that woman do the right thing by turning in the $1,000?

How Paul Defines Integrity

According to a report of this story in the *New York Times*, all 15 children said the woman was a fool. Later the *Times* reporter asked the teacher, "Why didn't you tell those kids that turning in the money was the right thing to do?" The teacher responded, "That is not my job. My job is simply to help them find truth as they find it within themselves."[1]

We can only wish that teacher lots of luck as she tries to help students "find truth as they find it within themselves." What pupils across America are much more likely to find are excuses to cheat, by copying answers from each other or copying entire pages from books and turning them in as their own work. One recent study of high school students showed 75 percent of them cheat on exams with the express purpose of "getting good enough grades to get into a good college." And, many blatantly claim it doesn't bother them at all. Their motto is, "Why flunk when you can cheat?"[2]

Are Christians Taking the Easy Road, Too?

It's not hard to find fault with secular society, but just how is integrity doing in the Church? Sociologist Tony Campolo charges that biblical Christianity has all but disappeared from North America. He believes we have been seduced into practicing a form of religiosity that is comfortable, entertaining, politically conservative and theologically naive, but in many ways a denial of what Jesus taught.[3]

Campolo goes on to accuse the American clergy of selling out by teaching a comfortable and unpainful form of Christianity in order to keep their memberships. An ordained Baptist minister, Campolo refers to an unspoken acknowledgment among the clergy to not ask people to take the Sermon on the Mount seriously for fear of losing members to other churches where discipleship is practiced on the broadest, easiest road possible. "We forget," says Campolo, "what Jesus said about broad and easy roads."[4]

Tony Campolo is well-known as a provocative speaker and teacher in Christian settings of all kinds. His strong words may poke holes in your comfort zone. It is useful, however, to simply ask, "Is he right about my church? Is he right about me? If our pastor started preaching on more sacrifice, would I move down the street to a church where I felt more comfortable? Does God want me to feel more comfortable? Or does He want me to feel more concern for the needs around me? Am I letting God work within me? How can I tell if I have real integrity?"

According to the dictionary, integrity is "the state of being unimpaired; soundness, completeness and unity." Synonyms for integrity are honesty, which implies truthfulness, and fairness, which means dealing without fraud or deceit. Integrity is a moral soundness that comes out in situations that test your steadfastness to truth, purpose, responsibility or trust.

In his letter to the Philippians, Paul doesn't use the word *integrity* directly, but that is what he is talking about when he makes a perfect capsule summary of living the Christian life in Philippians 2:12,13: "Therefore, my dear friends, as you have always obeyed . . . continue to work out your salvation with fear and trembling, for it is God who works in you to will and to act according to his good purpose."

In Philippians 2:12-18 Paul lists what could be called five signs of Christian integrity—proofs that your salvation is real and that you are interested in more than comfort, conformity and being entertained. To check for these signs, you need to ask yourself some hard questions:

Am I Making Any Progress? Are my old habits, faults or hang-ups fading and being replaced by new habits or practices that strengthen my Christian walk? How do I spend my time, money and energy? On myself? On God's Word? On people who need Him?

In verse 12 Paul mentions the obedience the Philippians have displayed in the past and he urges them to continue by working out their salvation with fear and trembling as they let God work within.

In Philippians 2:12, Paul is repeating the same idea he teaches in Ephesians 2:8-10. We don't work *for* our salvation, but we do work it *out* as we live the new life given to

us by Christ and then spend ourselves in helping others
(see Eph. 2:10). After all, if we have God's grace within
us, we agree it should come out and be seen in our lives.

Paul understands. In that short phrase with "fear and
trembling," he catches the essence of living from the
inside out. There are easier ways to live—not as fulfilling
or satisfying—but easier.

One of these "easy ways" *is to live on the outside and
never really look in.* We skim the surface of life, go through
the motions and seldom wrestle with the question that is
never far away: Who am I really?

The other easy, but even more unsatisfying, way to
live is *on the inside but seldom venturing out.* For the one
who lives on the inside, asking questions like: Who am I?
is no problem. We conduct daily introspective drills in re-
examining our motives, second-guessing our convictions
and lashing ourselves for not doing the good works God
has had ready since eternity past.

We want to be out there—joyfully sharing, loving,
accepting, working for His good pleasure—but we seldom
seem to pull it off. It is easier to stay inside—not really
that comfortable, but safer. And why change uncomfortable behavior if it's at least familiar—and safer, too?

Fortunately, there is one other option that is not that
easy or that comfortable. It involves growth and change
and takes us to our next question about integrity.

Is Christ Really My King and My Lord? How do I rec-
ognize the lordship of Jesus Christ in my life? Do I seek
Him out because I realize I cannot live without Him? I can
exist, yes, but live with integrity, no.

When Paul talks about working out our salvation with
fear and trembling, what does he mean? We must realize
Paul isn't talking about cowering before a judgmental and

vengeful God who is out to get us if we don't perform according to specifications. J.B. Phillips stresses in verse 12, to be keener than ever to "complete the salvation that God has given you with a proper sense of awe and responsibility."

In 1 Timothy 6:15,16, Paul gives the best description of the God we serve in awe and with responsibility: "the blessed and only Ruler, the King of kings and Lord of lords, who alone is immortal and who lives in unapproachable light, whom no one has seen or can see. To Him be honor and might forever. Amen."

Part of making Christ your Lord and King is to remember your Christian life did not start with you, it started with God. You didn't find God; He found you. You didn't wake up one morning, look in the mirror and say, "Hmmm, looks as if I need salvation—I'd better dash right over to heaven and get my share." *God woke you up*—out of spiritual slumber, actually spiritual death, and you came alive to what He had for you (see Eph. 2:1-9, 5:8-14; Col. 2:13).

And living from the inside out doesn't continue through our own efforts either. *God keeps us going.* The only reason we can work out our own salvation is that God is at work within us, giving us "the will and the power to achieve his purpose" (Phil. 2:13, *Phillips*). In typical fashion, Paul now adds some practical examples of how to work out your salvation as you let God work within.

Am I Easy to Live With? Paul's advice is to "do everything without complaining or arguing" (v. 14). When Paul speaks of complaining he is talking about a rebellious, even mutinous, attitude. The word he uses for *arguing* means "useless and often ill-natured debating or doubting."

Some good questions to ask ourselves are: How often

do I criticize, complain, grumble or argue? How often do I
use my "honesty" to cut people down and blow them
away? How often do I really give my opinions on everyone
and everything, without regard to the possible conse-
quences.

This kind of attitude can easily lead to gossip, backbiting and spreading rumors. Many Christian pastors and
leaders have felt the sting of gossip circulated about their
"divorce" or "affair" that never happened. It is so easy to
get on the phone and grumble and mumble about the pastor and the elders, the Sunday School superintendent—
and don't forget the choir director who seems to give too
big a smile to the organist. It's easy to play these games,
but it is not integrity.

Am I Making an Honest Effort? In Philippians 2:15
Paul gets to the bedrock of how a Christian is to live from
the inside out. A life of integrity is one that is "blameless
and pure . . . without fault in a crooked and depraved generation." Paul isn't talking about being perfect or flawless;
he's talking about making that honest effort every day to
tell the truth, not cheat or take advantage.

But life has a way of closing in, not with a rush or a
deafening roar, but subtly, quietly and expediently. Consider these "from real life" case studies:

> You are a foreman for a printing company and
> learn that next week your shift will start print-
> ing a porno-type newspaper. What do you do?

> You have just come through the line at the
> supermarket and discovered that the checker
> gave you too much change. She is very busy
> with another customer. What do you do?

You teach high school biology and your principal orders you to stop talking about Creation or your Christian faith when any students ask you. What can you do?

You are a married seminary student who works the night shift at a factory to pay the bills. But you need to spend tonight studying for a big exam or you'll probably fail. Should you call in "sick"?

Integrity is that quality within that gets tested in the fire—when the heat is on and you learn how strong your convictions about being pure and blameless really are.

Am I Sharing the Word of Life? A result of being blameless, pure and without fault, is to "shine like stars in the universe as you hold out the word of life" (Phil. 2:15,16). To sing: "This little light of mine—I'm going to let it shine," is not mouthing Sunday School platitudes. To live as a shining light is the awesome responsibility and challenge to every Christian given by Jesus Himself: "You are the light of the world . . . let your light shine before men, that they may see your good deeds and praise your Father in heaven" (Matt. 5:14,16).

Gene Getz, author of *Sharpening the Focus of the Church*, and director of the Center for Biblical Renewal, adds "The dynamic Christian life-style builds bridges to the world for verbal communication of the Gospel."[5] Dr. Getz believes that Christians shine best not as individual stars but in clusters, which emphasizes the need for love and unity that Paul has already talked about (see Phil. 2:1-4,14).

If Christians are going to hold forth the Word of life with integrity, they have to start in their own backyards. Within the Body of Christ, backbiting, second-guessing, gossiping, quibbling, pouting, sulking, adultery, lying and cheating have got to go. When believers can practice the kind of integrity that enables them to be blameless and pure, they will get the attention of a warped and crooked world, which casts a baleful eye on the scandals of televangelists and the growing number of Christian leaders who are becoming affair and divorce statistics.

With every Christian, integrity is Job One and it begins at the very personal and individual level. One writer describes integrity as pursuing "the truth wherever and whenever we find it, standing our ground even if no one else follows. It means avoiding the little white lie, not accepting the status quo, and not repeating the unsubstantiated rumor."

These are words, not from a theological journal or a daily devotional but from a newsletter going to business executives and managers interested in motivating their employees. Nonetheless, these words are as true for a Christian as they are for any executive driven by the thirst for success. This same article closes by asking a provocative question: "What would happen if significant numbers of people were to act with integrity just once more each day? The rallying effect would be magnificent. Even such a modest increase in the level of integrity could conceivably transform our society."[6]

Try changing that quote and inserting the word *Christians* for *people* and the words *the church* for *our society*. Think about it often as you continue to work out your own salvation with a proper sense of awe and responsibility, knowing that it is God who works within you, giving you the will and the strength to have integrity.

THE MORE
YOU SPEND
INTEGRITY,

THE MORE
YOU HAVE!

Like any Christian value, integrity must remain active and living. You have to display it again and again or you lose it. But the more you spend integrity, the more you have. Every time you act with integrity, you increase your chances of acting with more integrity the next time you face a decision to cop out, lie, cheat, be unfair or disloyal.

Paul never met Madame Chiang Kai-shek—at least in this life—but he would have liked the words she used to describe integrity:

> In the end, we are all the sum total of our actions. Character can't be counterfeited, nor

can it be put on and cast off as if it were a gar-
ment to meet the whim of the moment . . . Day
by day, we write our own destiny; for inexora-
bly . . . we become what we do.[7]

The following questions are designed for your personal
study or to discuss with a group. Record your answers in
your journal/notebook.

1. Reread the criticisms of the church by Tony Campolo
   under the subhead "Are Christians Taking the Easy
   Road, Too?" Then answer the questions that appear
   in that section. What does it mean for a Christian to
   have "real integrity"?

2. Review the definition of integrity in this chapter. Then
   compare it to the following Scripture passages: Leviti-
   cus 19:35; Proverbs 11:3, 19:1; Romans 12:17, 13:8.
   Which passages apply best to your life?

3. For some Old Testament accounts of integrity, see
   Moses' encounter with Korah and other Levites in
   Numbers 16:1-50; Samuel's confrontation of the Isra-
   elites in his farewell speech in which he asks them to
   find fault in his ministry, 1 Samuel 12:1-25; Elisha's
   encounter with Naaman after Naaman is healed of lep-
   rosy and Elisha refuses to accept any gifts, 2 Kings
   5:1-27. Note also what happens to Gehazi, Elisha's

servant, when he takes gifts from Naaman. What do these three stories tell you about integrity?

4. In Philippians 2:12 is Paul suggesting that you can earn your salvation? (see also Eph. 2:8-10). For you, which would be worse: Living on the outside and never looking in, or living on the inside but seldom venturing out? Why? Which translation of Philippians 2:12 is clearer? Why do you think so?

"Continue to work out your salvation with fear and trembling" (*NIV*).

"Complete the salvation that God has given you with a proper sense of awe and responsibility"(*Phillips*).

5. Which of the following phrases best describe God as you picture Him or seem to experience Him?

_____ Good buddy   _____ Demanding employer

_____ Kindly grandpa   _____ Encouraging coach

_____ Distant friend   _____ Strict parent

Why does 1 Timothy 6:15,16 give a better description than any of those above?

6. Do you agree or disagree with the statement: "Part of making Christ your Lord and King is to remember your Christian life did not start with you, it started with God. You didn't find God, He found you." See Ephesians 2:1-9, 5:8-14; Colossians 2:13; then write a paragraph in reaction to this statement.

7. In Philippians 2:14 Paul advises Christians to "do everything without complaining or arguing." Why is this difficult for so many believers? What can you do about it?

8. Philippians 2:15 tells us to live a life that is "blameless and pure." Is Paul asking Christians to be perfect? Why or why not?

9. Why is integrity so important in holding forth the Word of Life? (see Phil. 2:16).

10. Reread the real life case studies, which all deal with tests of integrity. How would you act in each case and why?

11. In your opinion, what would happen if significant numbers of Christians were to act with integrity just once more each day? Write a paragraph that describes the possibilities as you see them.

12. According to this chapter what is the way to have more and more integrity? Do you agree? Why or why not?

13. Reread the statement by Madame Chiang Kai-shek, which closes this chapter. Which phrases stand out for you? How do her thoughts compare to Philippians 2:12,13?

Taking Stock and Setting Goals

1. To test your integrity, take the following quiz and give yourself points as follows: 5 = always; 4 = often, 3 = sometimes; 2 = occasionally; 1 = never.

a. I am honest and forthright.
b. I give any job or assignment my all.
c. I am loyal and devoted to my church.
d. I keep my word.
e. "Totally committed" describes me.
f. I faithfully nurture my devotional life.
g. I work out my salvation with a proper sense of awe and responsibility.
h. I resist being critical, complaining or contentious.
i. My life is blameless and pure.
j. I share the Word of Life with others.

Scoring: 40-50 = excellent, you are definitely living from the inside out. 30-39 = good . . . . but ask God to show you areas for improvement. 0-29 = poor, you and the Lord need to talk.

2. Areas where I plan to work on having more integrity:
Honesty
Tithes and offerings
Complaining and arguing (gossiping)
Witness and testimony
Doing what I say I believe
Other: _____

3. Specific goals I have set regarding increasing my integrity: _____

Lord, having integrity isn't easy

It's easier to tell white lies, to fudge a little on the taxes or the expense account, to call in sick when all I'm sick of is work. It's easier to put on a front and wear a mask of respectability. Help me remember integrity isn't something I wear, it's something I am. Thank you, Lord, for working in my life to rip *off* the counterfeit and put *in* the real thing.

Notes

1. Quoted by Charles Colson in "The Secularization of America," *Discipleship Journal*, Issue 38, 1987, p. 41.
2. See "High School Test Cheating: 75 Percent Admit It, Cite Pressure," David G. Savage, *Los Angeles Times*, Thursday, April 17, 1986, Part 1, p. 3; and "Cheating: Just Part of the Game," *San Diego Tribune*, Nov. 24, 1986, p. 1 of the "Scene" section.
3. Tony Campolo, "The Demise of Evangelicalism," *Discipleship Journal*, Issue 39, 1987, p. 18.
4. Ibid.
5. Gene A. Getz, *Pressing On When You'd Rather Turn Back* (Ventura, CA: Regal Books, 1985), p. 103.
6. Jeffrey P. Davidson, "Integrity: The Vanishing Virtue," *P.M.A. Advisor*, Vol. 5, No. 9, © 1986, W. Clement Stone P.M.A. Communications, Inc., Sept. 1986.
7. Quoted by William Nichols, *A Treasury of Words to Live By* (New York: Simon & Schuster, Inc., 1947), p. 14.

CHAPTER SIX

WHAT DID PAUL VALUE MOST OF ALL?

SELF...
RIGHTEOUSNESS

Zermatt, Switzerland was a lovely, idyllic village at the foot of the Matterhorn. Cars could not climb the steep grade to Zermatt, and the only way in was by cogwheel railroad. The villagers valued their life-style, which was peaceful, untouched by the outside world. They also valued their water supply, which came cold, clear and pure from glaciers high in the mountains.

And then disaster struck. Cases of typhoid broke out everywhere, and an epidemic raged. When the source of the disease was discovered, authorities learned that the water main passing through town had a crack in it. Animal refuse from farmers' fields had seeped into that crack, typhoid bacillus had started to breed and the pipe had become contaminated. What the villagers had thought was the purest, clearest water on earth, was actually killing them.[1]

As Paul moves on in Philippians chapter 3, he talks about something he values above all else—the righteousness he has in Jesus Christ. Before Paul met Jesus in a blinding flash of light at the Damascus city limits, he worked tirelessly for the perfect relationship with God. But as Saul the Pharisee, he never really found peace, because he tried to quench his spiritual thirst at a contaminated source.

Perhaps that explains why he persecuted the young Christian church so viciously. After holding the coats of those who stoned Stephen and watching the Apostle die serenely, Paul stormed off to Damascus to round up more

Christians. He was sure he could win more brownie points with God by persecuting this pesky new "cult." Instead, he wound up literally coming down from his high horse, looking up out of the dirt and asking Jesus, "Lord, what do you want me to do?"

At that moment Paul's entire value system turned upside down. He drank deeply from his Lord's "spring of living water," which gave him the peace of mind and soul he had sought all his life. Paul went on to become a crusader against the things he once thought valuable—even priceless. Righteousness achieved by human effort alone became cursed in his sight.

The contaminated pipe that was killing the villagers of Zermatt is a graphic picture of the human righteousness that Paul renounced. No matter how "good" we think we are (especially in comparison to others), we are still like that pipe. We may do good deeds, even act out of pure love and devotion to God, but without Christ we are still contaminated by sin. We are spiritually dead, but don't know it.

Requiem for a Pharisee

As Paul writes to the Philippians, he recalls that his performance as a Pharisee was "faultless" (see Phil. 3:6; some translations say "blameless"). If righteousness could have been gained by obeying the rules and living by the book, he had been the most righteous man who ever lived.

The Greek word Paul uses for faultless refers in particular to avoiding sins of omission. As far as the Law was concerned, *Paul had left nothing undone.* That particular record was spotless and beyond any criticism. [2]

It's not typical for someone to reel off his pedigree and then reject all of it as worthless, but that's just what Paul does. What he valued and thought profitable before—his birthright as a Jew and his training as a Pharisee—is now worthless and unprofitable. Why?

Before meeting Christ, Paul had a view of righteousness that emphasized conforming to a certain standard— the Law. But while Paul assured himself of his righteousness, the gnawing uncertainty and discontent were always there.

In spite of all his learning, Paul was guilty of the same mistake made by all the Pharisees. They became so preoccupied with tiny details of right and wrong and scrupulous obedience to ceremonial ritual and regulations, that they drifted far from the great principles taught in the Old Testament. That's why Christ told the Pharisees they were tithing a tenth of their spices but neglecting the far weightier matters of justice, mercy and faithfulness (see Matt. 23:23).

In His Sermon on the Mount, Jesus taught: "For I tell you that unless your righteousness surpasses that of the Pharisees and the teachers of the law, you will certainly not enter the kingdom of heaven" (5:20). Jesus wasn't changing the game plan; *He was simply clarifying what the plan had always been from the beginning.* Instead of putting the emphasis on the external—ritual and legalism—the follower of God is to put emphasis on the internal—faith and obedience. Righteousness comes only through God's grace, responding to faith in the heart of the believer (see Gen. 15:6, Rom. 4:13).

Paul held many Christian values but the pearl of greatest price for Paul was *Christ Himself.* That's why he considers everything loss compared to knowing Christ for "whose sake I have lost all things" (Phil. 3:8). Paul not only wanted to gain Christ, he wanted to "be found in him, not having a righteousness of my own that comes from the law, but that which is through faith in Christ—the righteousness that comes from God and is by faith" (v. 9).

Do We Take Righteousness for Granted?

A key to understanding just how much Paul valued Christ is to look more closely at why he calls all the results of human effort and motive, "rubbish"(v. 8). All kinds of rubbish—the Greek word literally means "excrement"—can crowd into our lives and tempt us to devalue Christ with our thoughts, words and actions. Instead of treating Jesus like a pearl of great price or a 10-carat diamond, we may act as though He is no more than a zirconia, or a piece of cheap rhinestone jewelry.

In a song he made popular in the 1970s, country singer Glen Campbell told the story of the "Rhinestone Cowboy" and the "load of compromisin'" he would have to do "on the way to his horizon." But compromising didn't matter; what counted for him was that he was going to be "where the lights are shinin' on me."

There are many ways to clutter our lives with the rubbish of compromise. We live in a materialistic culture that teaches everyone that living well means purchasing and owning things. Research studies point out that by the time teenagers graduate from high school, they will have seen hundreds of thousands of TV commercials, most of which tell them that if they can just buy the right car, home, toothpaste or item of personal hygiene, their problems will vanish and life will become beautiful.

"Consumer, Come into My Parlor"

Materialism is like a giant spider's web. We are easily and inevitably lured into the spider's parlor as we live by slo-

gans that all boil down to "I am what I own," while we hum, "Let the good times roll"

Particularly in America, the church has not escaped materialism—in fact, many believers have embraced it. In *Will Evangelicalism Survive Its Own Popularity?* Jon Johnston observes that American Christians have joined their non-Christian neighbors in wasting everything from fuel and food to millions of dollars spent on clothes, cars and "cathedral-like buildings" that glorify men, not God. [3] Some branches of Christianity actually reach out and embrace materialism by preaching a gospel of prosperity with their exhortations to name it and claim it.

The simple answer to materialism would seem to be developing a more simplistic life-style, but even here it is easy to miss the mark. In *Defeating the Dragons of the World*, Stephen Eyre confesses that he practiced the gospel of simple living by righteously refusing to buy a washer and dryer, even though his wife struggled with two children in diapers. Apparently, they were cloth diapers because no sincere believer in the gospel of simple living would think of using Pampers. Eyre's wife was spending every other day at the laundromat until some family friends stepped in with a little friendly advice.

Eyre finally realized he was practicing his own form of materialism as he measured his spirituality, as well as that of other Christians, by how much or how little they owned. He saw that being spiritual versus being materialistic is not determined by owning or not owning certain things. What is crucial is whether or not the things own you.

Whether we are trying to acquire too much or live on less, we can get preoccupied with the physical side of life. Instead of living from the inside out, we become preoccupied with the outside. The result is that the reality of a life of righteousness in Christ becomes hollow and tasteless. We end up keeping God at a distance as we hide behind our clutter and rubbish.

But What Will People Think?

Materialism leads naturally to another form of compromise—trying to live up to the expectations of the peer group. We cater to the crowd, the nameless, faceless ones who control our lives as we constantly wonder, "What will *they* think of me and my family?" Conformism is what makes us run after the latest fashion and throw away perfectly good clothes because some all-knowing designer decides hemlines should go up or down or that ties should become narrow or wide.

Conformism strikes its most deadly blows, however, through the pressure of the peer group. Adults chide teenagers for going along with the crowd but the teenagers are only doing what they see the adults model in more subtle ways. No matter how old or young we are, we want to be "in," we want to be accepted. We don't enjoy scorn or being laughed at.

We even conform to avoid sticky or unpleasant situations with our friends. We may not tell an outright lie but we adjust the truth a bit, or say nothing when we are thinking thoughts that don't agree at all with the drift of the conversation. We are, in effect "more concerned about what we think others want to hear than about speaking the truth."[4]

Like materialism, conformism has invaded and infected the Church. When he was ordained, Stephen Eyre received a gift copy of *The Holy Fool*, a novel about a pastor who wound up faking the role of a "sanctified Christian

leader" after losing his faith. Eyre wasn't sure if the book was a subtle hint or a blatant warning, but it made him realize that by fearing what others think and conforming to what we think others want us to be and do, "we can become performers in a holy play before the church and world."[5]

Eyre is thankful for his small group and prayer partners who help him with being honest rather than being tempted to project the image of "Christian leader with no problems." When he pontificates or starts to sound overconfident, his group asks him, "Come on, how is it really going?" Without his group, Eyre is sure that he would be

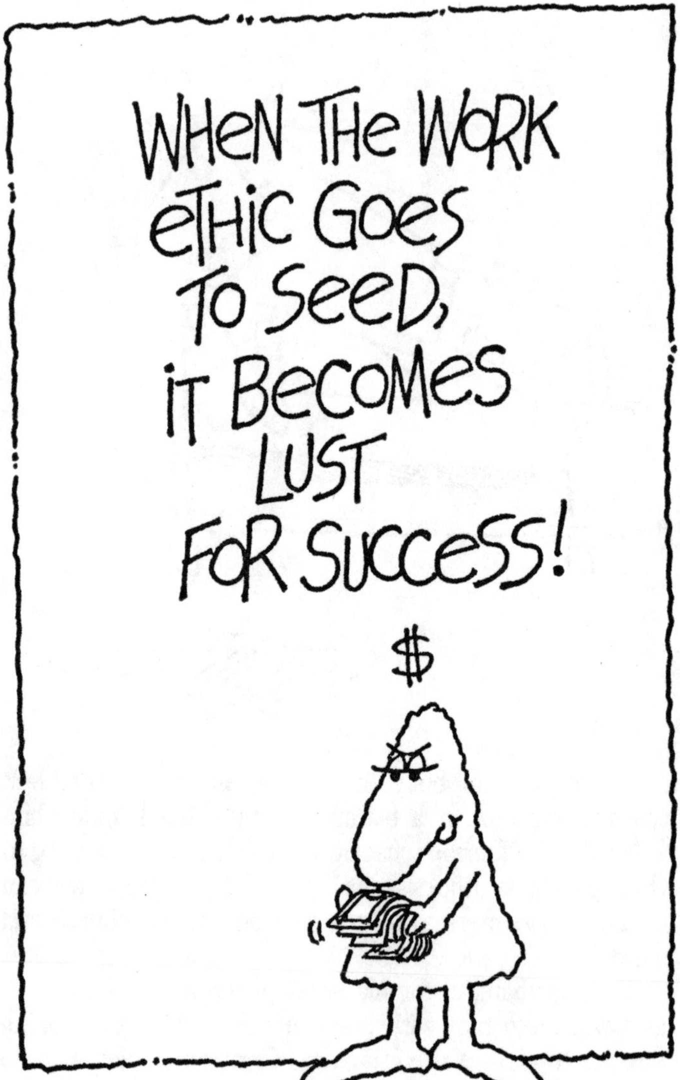
WHEN THE WORK
ETHIC GOES
TO SEED,
IT BECOMES
LUST
FOR SUCCESS!
$

"condemned to spiritual superficiality; keeping up an image that would put a wall between me and the fellowship that I need."[6]

Beware of the Barrenness of Busyness

While getting hung up on things and the opinions of others are both dangerous, there is yet another kind of rubbish that can pile up in our lives and corrode the very vitals of our relationship to God in Christ. Paul knew from experience there is no more deadly foe of true Christianity than *works*. And we should heed his warning because there is no greater hotbed of success mania and glorification of working hard and hustling than our American culture. Americans pride themselves in their so-called work ethic, but when the work ethic goes to seed, it becomes lust for success and wanting to win at any price.

Go into any bookstore and you can learn how to win through intimidation, develop a winning attitude, even eat to win. It is no wonder that terms like *stressed out* and *burned out* have become common in our vocabularies over the last 10 years. "Going for the jugular" is just plain hard work. Having or doing it all is bound to lead to exhaustion.

Many Christians rationalize that they aren't guilty of the gross sins involved with winning, but they slip and slide on the rubbish of busyness and works just the same. Churches are full of tired Christians who feel overworked and underappreciated, who wonder why the core group has to do all the Sunday School teaching, all the cooking for the socials, all the telephoning . . .

When Satan ensnares Christians in a subtle form of works by getting them extra busy for God, he has them just where he wants them. We can clutter our lives by cluttering our schedules with far more activities than we could ever possibly cover. Meanwhile, we neglect the greater things and the more goodly portion—time in the Word and conversations with Christ on more than a hit-or-miss basis. We become victims of busyness, workaholism and keeping our ever-present schedule and to-do lists. We quote John 3:16 and Ephesians 2:8,9 but we live by the mottos: "I am what I do" or "I am what I produce."

Do You Know Why Christ Saved You?

In his portrait of *The Adequate Man*, which he draws from his comprehensive exposition of Philippians, Paul S. Rees asks, "If you are a Christian today, do you know why Christ seized you in His love and saved you by His grace? Are you quite sure?"[7]

Like many Christians, says Rees, we might answer by saying, "Of course, I know—to save me from hell" or we might say, "To rid me of my guilt." Or perhaps we would be positive and say, "To make me a new and different person."

Rees believes that if Paul were listening, he would simply shake his head. All these things are good and desirable, but they aren't the real reason Christ has redeemed us. The real reason is tucked in a tiny phrase in Philippians 3:10. Christ saved you and me so we could *know Him.* Not his gifts, blessings or benefits, but Him and the "power of his resurrection . . . the fellowship of sharing in his sufferings."

The world has not known a more powerful witness for Jesus Christ than the apostle Paul. Yet here, in the twilight of his career, under house arrest and chained to a Roman guard, Paul wanted even more of the cleansing power of Christ that can destroy sin, make him more holy and even more effective as a witness.

Paul wants a new measure of the same kind of power that raised Christ from the dead. Why? So he can feel good and be happy? So he can be blessed, sustained and protected in times of trouble? No. Paul wants this power in order *to share with Christ in His sufferings*!

In Paul's mind, no sacrifice or effort is too great if it is made for Jesus Christ. Christ is why Paul was willing to give up everything else in order to be completely holy. Paul wants to be conformed to His death (see Phil. 3:10). What Paul means here is better explained in a closely paralleled passage, Romans 6:4-11, where he talks about becoming dead to sin. Paul wants to be dead to selfishness and self-centeredness, to be a blessing to others just as Christ was in His death.[8]

And what is the bottom line to all this? Why does Paul want the power of Christ's resurrection, the fellowship of His sufferings and conformity to His death? "In order that I may attain to the resurrection from the dead" (Phil. 3:11, *NASB*).

Some commentators think Paul wanted martyrdom and to somehow rise from the dead just as Christ did. Others speculate that Paul may have been simply speaking out of a sense of humility and unworthiness. Whatever Paul meant, he is not doubting his salvation (see 1 Tim. 1:12), or the fact that someday the dead in Christ would be raised—including him (see 1 Cor. 15:53,54). Perhaps Ken Taylor's paraphrase of Philippians 3:11 comes closest: "So, whatever it takes, I will be one who lives in the fresh newness of life of those who are alive from the dead."

Paul valued his perfect relationship to God through faith so much that he made his life purpose knowing Christ and the fellowship of His sufferings. Can we persevere to the same end? That is our question in the next chapter.

The following questions are designed for your personal study or to discuss with a group. Record your answers in your journal/notebook.

1. Reread the story of Zermatt, Switzerland's typhoid epidemic. Suppose someone would argue, "But if they had tried hard enough they could have kept contamination out of the water pipe. The typhoid was caused by a human error, but it doesn't prove that man is inherently sinful." What would you say?

2. Before reading this chapter, would you have named righteousness in Christ a Christian value? Would it have ranked in your top three? Why or why not?

3. What causes Paul to list his many credentials as a pure blooded Jew and a former Pharisee? (see Phil. 3:5,6). Who is Paul talking about in Philippians 3:3,4? (see also Acts 15:1-11; Gal. 2:1-5, 6:12-15). Why does he call them dogs?

4. Why does Paul dismiss his spotless pedigree as a Jew and a Pharisee as "rubbish"? (see Phil. 3:7-9). Try paraphrasing these verses and putting yourself in Paul's place. What have you lost for the sake of Christ? What have you gained?

5. According to this chapter, where did the Pharisees go wrong? Is it possible for Christians to drift into error

just as the Pharisees did? In what way might this happen?

6. Do you agree or disagree with the statement: "Instead of treating Jesus like a pearl of great price or a 10-carat diamond, we may act as though He is no more than a zirconia, or a piece of cheap rhinestone jewelry." Why?

7. Why is it so easy in America—or any number of other prosperous countries—to start believing, "I am what I own"?

8. Write your own definition of *materialism*; then compare it to the Stephen Eyre story of how he refused to buy a washer and dryer for his wife because he thought it was spiritual to let her haul diapers to the laundromat. What did Eyre finally realize that helped him see the difference between *spiritual* and *materialistic*?

9. Reread the material under the subhead, "But What Will People Think?" and list several ways we fall victim to conformism. Which of these are a problem for you?

10. At what point does busyness turn into barrenness? When can the work ethic go to seed? Do you see this happening in your own life?

11. Do you agree or disagree: "When Satan ensnares Christians in a subtle form of works by getting them extra busy for God, he has them just where he wants them"? What about all the Christians who aren't busy for God at all? Won't God have a special reward for those who work extra hard?

12. In this chapter, a quote from Paul S. Rees asks, "If you are a Christian today, do you know why Christ seized you in His love and saved you by His grace? Are you quite sure?" What is your answer to Dr. Rees's question? What is Paul's answer? (see Phil. 3:10).

13. What two life purposes has Paul chosen? (see Phil. 3:10,11). Why does he want to know Christ? Why does he want to become like Him in His death?

14. How does Philippians 3:10,11 make you feel? Are you on Paul's wavelength? Do you want to be?

Taking Stock and Setting Goals

1. "Rubbish" that clutters my relationship to Christ includes:
   _____ Getting hung up on things, the physical side of life
   _____ Worrying about what people will think
   _____ Being busier than God wants me to be
   _____ Other: _____
   _____

2. I plan to do some "life cleaning" by doing the following:

3. My specific goals for knowing Christ better, according to Philippians 3:10,11, are: _____
   _____
   _____
   _____

Lord, what do I really value most?

When asked to list my priorities, I often write Christ or God at the top, followed by spouse, family, church, job, hobbies, etc. But you know my heart—much better than I do. You see me compromise in subtle ways—and some not so subtle. Forgive me, Lord, for being too distracted and too busy to appreciate the righteousness you provided. Above all, strengthen my will, which is overly influenced by my flesh. I want to know you and your power. Change me, Lord, and thanks for being patient.

Notes

1. James M. Boice, *Philippians: An Expositional Commentary* (Grand Rapids, MI: Zondervan Publishing House, 1982), p. 196.
2. William Barclay, *The Letters to Philippians, Colossians, Thessalonians, The Daily Study Bible* (Edinburgh: The St. Andrew Press, 1959), pp. 71-75.
3. Jon Johnston, *Will Evangelicalism Survive Its Own Popularity?* (Grand Rapids, MI: Zondervan Publishing House, 1980), pp. 86-95.
4. Stephen D. Eyre, *Defeating the Dragons of the World* (Downers Grove, IL: InterVarsity Press, 1959), p. 83.
5. Ibid., p. 86.
6. Ibid.
7. Paul S. Rees, *The Adequate Man* (Old Tappan, NJ: Fleming H. Revell Co, 1959), p. 74.
8. William Hendriksen, *New Testament Commentary, Exposition of Philippians* (Grand Rapids, MI: Baker Book House, 1979), pp. 168,169.

CHAPTER SEVEN

PRESS ON WITH A PURPOSE

What is your life purpose? Before you answer, think about John Goddard. As a teenager, Goddard kept hearing adults complaining, "Oh, if I had only done this or that when I was younger," and he purposed to not let life slip by him. He kept that vow, and at age 47 he was featured in *Life* magazine for completing 103 out of 127 goals he had spelled out for himself at age 15.

Life didn't do a feature story on John Goddard because he had reached goals like, "Own a BMW before I'm 21."

Goddard's goals, which eventually led to earning as much as $50,000 a year as an adventurer/lecturer, included exploring rivers like the Nile, Amazon and Congo, and climbing mountains like the Matterhorn, Kilimanjaro, McKinley and Fuji.

By 1972, he had landed on and taken off from an aircraft carrier, had made a parachute jump, had learned to fence and had mastered jujitsu. He also had written a book (on a trip up the Nile), and had learned French, Spanish and Arabic. In addition, he had read the entire *Encyclopedia Britannica*, plus the Bible, and had gone on a mission for his church.[1]

I called John Goddard recently and learned that he has checked off four more of the 127 goals he set as a teenager: visits to the Great Wall of China, Easter Island and the Galapagos Islands, plus learning to play polo. He told me that since making his original list, he has set and reached many additional goals, including becoming one of the few civilians to ever pilot an F-111 fighter at 1500 mph. Now in his 60s, Goddard maintains a steady speaking and lecturing schedule, living life as zestfully as ever.

For sheer quantity, John Goddard ranks right up there in setting and reaching goals. But for sheer quality, someone from more ancient history has the edge. The apostle Paul also did a lot of traveling, became proficient in many languages, wrote several books and went on several church missions of his own.

But his chief purpose in life was the greatest of all. In chapter 6 we saw how Saul the Pharisee, became Paul the Apostle with an entirely new perspective on how to gain righteousness.

How changed are my ambitions! thought Saul. "Now I long to know Christ and the power shown by his resurrection: now I long to share his sufferings" (Phil. 3:10, *Phillips*).

That lofty life purpose determined every goal Paul set, and Paul set and reached a lot of them. Almost single-handedly, he introduced Christianity to his known civilized world. Paul lived long before goal-setting seminars and managing by objectives became popular, but he could have held his own with any hard-driving executive, and then some.

Perseverance Kept Paul Going

Along with goal setting, Paul valued perseverance. In fact, his lofty purpose to know Christ and His sufferings and make Him Lord across the world would never have been fulfilled without the perseverance that kept him pressing on to finish his race.

No matter how much Paul accomplished, or how much he learned, he never thought he had it made or that he knew it all. Instead, he spoke of how "I press on to take hold of that for which Christ Jesus took hold of me . . . . I press on toward the goal to win the prize for which God has called me heavenward in Christ Jesus" (vv. 12,14).

Paul loved athletic metaphors and obviously had seen more than one Olympic contest, probably in Greece where the Olympic games rivaled those held in Rome. That's why Paul could say that he was to forget what is behind and strain toward what is ahead. Here he pictures the runner straining toward his goal to win his prize. Paul saw his life as a race—a race run for Christ. But it was no 100-yard dash. Paul knew he was in the ultra marathon of them all—taking up his cross daily and following Christ for the rest of his life.

IS WHAT I BELIEVE IN BIG ENOUGH TO PULL THE BEST OUT OF ME?

In *A Long Obedience in the Same Direction*, Eugene Peterson notes that people get interested in the gospel, but find it extremely hard to stay interested. Millions make decisions for Christ, but there is a "dreadful attrition rate. Many claim to have been born again, but the evidence for mature Christian discipleship is slim."

A lot of believers are in the market for religious experience and ecstacy, but there is less demand for the hard work involved in knowing Christ and the power of His resurrection. As Peterson puts it, there is "little inclination to sign up for a long apprenticeship in what earlier generations of Christians called holiness."[2]

In short, many of us are good starters but find it hard to keep going. We have made the team but we don't always make the grade. We understand Paul's frequent reference to athletics and the need for discipline, but we prefer hearing about how God works for our good in all things rather than learning how we can work for His glory in all things.

Paul, however, was a forerunner of the slogan found in so many fitness centers today: No pain, no gain. When facing those inevitable times when it seems you are falling back or even ready to drop out of the race, it's time to reexamine your purpose. Ask yourself, "Is what I believe in big enough to pull the best out of me?"

He Lost His Feet, but Gained a Purpose

After a gridiron career that included winning all-American honors at Baylor University and all-pro defensive end status with the Cleveland Browns, Bill Glass dedicated his life to helping people develop winning attitudes and habits by relating to Jesus Christ. While on a speaking tour, Glass shared a story he had heard about a man who had run a marathon without any feet! He had never stopped once, running the entire 26-mile race on the stubs of his ankles, which were cushioned by foam rubber.

What Bill Glass didn't realize was that in his audience was a former football player who had been a Number Two draft choice with the San Diego Chargers as a kicking specialist. Dale Edison had spent his life kicking a football, first over a bench as a little fellow, then over the fence and finally over the house. While attending San Diego State University, he kicked 20 consecutive field goals without a miss.

When he was drafted by the Chargers (the highest draft choice for any kicking specialist up to that time), he decided to celebrate with friends on the Fourth of July. What better way than to set off a big bang to match the one that he'd be making in the pros that fall? Edison and his friends stuffed all kinds of sulphur explosives into a milk can. Somebody lit the fuse and there was a freak explosion that took off both of Dale Edison's feet and one of his hands.

But Dale Edison hadn't given up. He was struggling with still trying to make something of his life, even though his football career was gone. He'd driven several hours to hear Glass speak that night and when the message was over, Dale was the first man to the front, walking on new artificial feet to meet and shake hands with Bill Glass.

Tears were streaming down Dale Edison's cheeks as he recalled the story of the marathon runner with no feet. "I'll never, never, never give up!" he promised Glass.

And he didn't. He went on to be a leader in his church and in business and civic life. He refused to let tragedy or adversity get him down. He just wouldn't quit. [3]

Dale Edison is a striking example of having a purpose big enough to actually affect what you do and how you live.

WHEN YOUR PURPOSE IS BIGGER THAN YOU ARE, YOU RISE TO NEW LEVELS OF ACHIEVEMENT.

When your purpose is bigger than you are, you rise to new levels of achievement that you never thought possible. You press on toward the mark—and you never give up.

Persevering Means Setting Goals

Vowing to never give up is where it all starts, but it takes perseverance and persistence to finish. The dictionary definition of *perseverance* says: "Holding to a course of action, belief or program without giving way." Holding to a course of action suggests making plans and setting goals that give specific reality to your purpose.

It is important to realize that a purpose is not quite the same as a goal. In *Strategy for Living*, Edward Dayton and Ted Engstrom describe a purpose as a general aim or direction we will want to take, while a goal is something in the future that we believe is measurable and accomplishable.[4]

To put it in terms of your devotional life, 2 Timothy 2:15 is a great purpose: "Do your best to present yourself to God as one approved, a workman who does not need to be ashamed and who correctly handles the word of truth." Reading the entire Bible through in a year and memorizing at least one verse from each book of the Bible during that time are measurable goals.

Your purpose sets your course. Your goals are measurable milestones to help you get there.

When you set goals, you suggest what might be accomplished. Goals are dreams and aspirations that are always fun to think about. But reaching goals—that's different. That takes sweat, hard work, hanging in there—discipline.

The number of goals you set should depend on what you feel fits your temperament, energy and life-style.

Goals should be just out of reach, but not out of sight. They should be challenging but not impossible. Your goals should get you going, but not weigh you down or discourage you.

Take care also to not have too many goals. John Goddard had 127 and seemed to live a challenging, fulfilled life. A lot of people would have trouble with 27 significant goals, or even seven.

That's why priorities are important. A priority is very close to a value—something that takes precedence in order of importance or urgency.

Urgency Can Be a Cruel Tyrant

In his classic booklet *The Tyranny of the Urgent,"* Charles Hummel develops the "constant tension between the urgent and the important."[5] Sometimes putting out fires—doing the urgent—is more fun and exciting than building or maintaining something that is really important but sometimes dull or routine. We can exist as slaves under the tyranny of the urgent rather than do the truly important.

For example, we usually nod in agreement when someone asks, Are Bible study and prayer important? But we can easily neglect both by substituting in its place "the urgent," like doing the dishes, cleaning the house, cooking the special dinner, attending the meeting or answering an important letter.

Living under the tyranny of the urgent often frustrates us in reaching our goals. At least, it can definitely get us sidetracked and have us neglect the important goals we have set to accomplish, change or create something significant in our lives that hasn't been there before.

How then can you prioritize your goals properly? One

standard approach recommended by many specialists is the A-B-C technique:

A = Must do or very high value

B = Should do or medium value

C = Can do or low value

The A-B-C technique is helpful but it is no magic wand. The first snag you may encounter is winding up with so many A goals you don't know which one to tackle first. Rather than deciding, it's easy to slip into that well-known state of agony called procrastination—when you perfect every stalling technique you can think of while getting nothing done.

The only way to battle procrastination is to take all your A goals and prioritize them: A-1, A-2 and so on. That way you can zero in on the one goal you want to accomplish first, do it, and then go on to the next. In this way, you perseverance isn't eroded by frustration or lack of focus.

Are You a Cheetah or a Sloth?

For sheer ability to focus on a goal, take a lesson from the cheetah, the big cat acknowledged as the swiftest of all four-footed animals. Cheetahs have been clocked at 70 miles an hour as they pursue their prey, and once they single out what they are after, nothing can detract them. The chase may lead past other animals the cheetah could catch much more easily, but he ignores them, intent only on reaching his primary goal.[6]

At the other end of the spectrum is the hapless sloth,

one of the world's slowest and dumbest creatures. He moves at about 14 feet per hour and is usually quite unaware of what's going on around him. He sleeps 18 hours out of every 24 and when attacked he can neither fight back or run away, and can only hope that his thick fur will somehow be a defense.

Paul's Plan for Procrastinators

Woven throughout Paul's writings to New Testament churches are suggestions that can become a plan for dealing with procrastination and slothfulness.

First, be sure to do something. Solomon advises, "Whatever your hand finds to do, do it with all your might" (Eccles. 9:10). He also observed that the lazy person wants much but gets little, while the diligent person prospers (see Prov. 13:4).

Paul told the Thessalonians, "For even when we were with you, we gave you this rule: 'If a man will not work, he shall not eat'" (2 Thess. 3:10). He also warned members of that same church, "let us not be like others, who are asleep, but let us be alert and self-controlled" (1 Thess. 5:6).

Next, be sure to do it now, not later. Some people excuse procrastination by saying they are waiting for the leading of the Lord. But as someone said, You can't guide a bicycle when it is parked. Paul always looked to God for guidance, but he was usually on the move and moving those around him into action as well with encouragement like: "Now it is high time to awake out of sleep" (Rom. 13:11, *NKJV*).

Solomon once walked by the field of a certain lazy fellow who lived by the motto, "I can do it later." The field was covered with thorns and weeds and the walls were broken down, and Solomon learned this lesson: "'A little extra sleep, a little more slumber, a little folding of the hands to rest' means that poverty will break in upon you suddenly like a robber, and violently like a bandit" (Prov. 24:32-34, *TLB*).

Most important, commit everything you do to the Lord. If your purpose is to know Him and the power of His resurrection, take Paul's advice: "Whatever your task is, put your whole heart and soul into it, as into work done for the Lord and not merely for men—knowing that your real reward will come from him" (Col. 3:23,24, *Phillips*).

Are You Using What You Already Know?

Procrastination and purposelessness are forms of immaturity, something that Paul mentions in Philippians 3:15 after urging his friends in Philippi to press on toward the goal to win the prize. Paul says, "All of us who are mature should take such a view of things. And if on some point you think differently, that too God will make clear to you. Only let us live up to what we have already attained" (Phil. 3:15,16).

The Living Bible paraphrases verse 16: "Fully obey the truth you have." Perhaps that sums it all up.

> Instead of looking for another new system or formula for success . . .

> Instead of hoping to find the answer in the latest best-seller from your favorite Christian guru . . .

> Instead of blaming the pastor for not preaching the sermons that are not practical enough . . .

Instead of knowing Christ secondhand by letting other people do your studying for you and then spoon-feeding you with a few swallows at a time . . .

Simply obey the truth you already have.

Has it ever occurred to you that most Christians already know far more than they are putting into practice? If Christianity is a long race of obedience in the same direction—and it is—then it's obvious what must be done.

The race is long and hot. The track can get rocky, full of potholes and even detours. But if we obey the truth we already have, we will receive power to finish the race and win the prize God is waiting to give us as we break the tape.

The following questions are designed for your personal study or to discuss with a group. Record your answers in your journal/notebook.

1. John Goddard set and reached over 100 significant goals during his lifetime. Take inventory on significant goals you have reached in your life and long-range goals you are still working on. Which ones involve your Christian faith and walk?

2. In Philippians 3:12, Paul says, "I press on to take hold of that for which Christ Jesus took hold of me." Why did He "take hold of" Paul? (see Acts 22:1-21, 26:1-23).

3. Describe in your own words the goal and prize at which Paul was aiming (see Phil. 3:14; see also 2 Tim. 4:6-8).

4. Do you agree or disagree with Eugene Peterson's statement: "Many claim to have been born again, but the evidence for mature Christian discipleship is slim"? What evidence do you see of mature discipleship in your own life?

5. Which of the following slogans best describe your Christian walk and why?

   a. No pain, no gain.

   b. It's Friday, but Sunday's comin.

   c. If it's to be, it's up to me.

6. According to this chapter, what is the difference between a purpose and a goal? Try writing down some of your purposes and goals.

7. Why should goals be "out of reach, but not out of sight"?

8. In your own life, how do you differentiate between the urgent and important? Should all urgent items be "A" priorities?

9. When it comes to battling procrastination, I am a __ cheetah; __ sloth; __ plow horse; __ race horse; __ other.

10. Which do you need to do more of in your own struggles with procrastination?

_____ Be sure to do something
_____ Commit what I do to the Lord
_____ Do it *now.*

Taking Stock and Setting Goals

1. My major purposes in life are:

2. My long-range (five years or more) goals are:

3. My goals for this coming year are:

4. My current goals are:

Lord, I want to persevere

Help me obey the truth I already have.

Notes
1. Richard Woodbury, "One Man's Life of No Regrets," *Life*, Mar. 24, 1972, p. 66.
2. Eugene H. Peterson, *A Long Obedience in the Same Direction* (Downers Grove, IL: InterVarsity Press, 1980), p. 12.
3. Bill Glass and James E. McEachen, *Plan to Win* (Waco, TX: Word, Inc., 1984), pp. 114-116.
4. Edward R. Dayton and Ted W. Engstrom, *Strategy for Living* (Ventura, CA: Regal Books, 1976), pp. 48-53.
5. Charles E. Hummel, *The Tyranny of the Urgent* (Downers Grove, IL: InterVarsity Press, 1967).
6. Paul Lee Tan, *Encyclopedia of 7700 Illustrations* (Garland, TX: Assurance Publishers, 1979), p. 138.

CHAPTER EIGHT

(HOW) NOT TO WORRY!

QUESTION: What is something few of us value but most of us tend to do too often?
ANSWER: WORRY

Worry and anxiety are called the most useless of emotions, but they dog our footsteps constantly. Pastors may even tells us it's a sin to worry—*that* really helps! Nationally known psychologist, Wayne Dyer, tell us things like: "You could take the ten best worriers in the entire world. Put them in the same room for the rest of their lives and allow them to worry and worry only. And you know what would happen? Absolutely nothing!"[1]

He may have something there. We know it's useless, and even harmful, to worry. Studies show that worry can actually cause disease, particularly in the digestive organs and the heart. So what can we do about worry, besides worrying about what it's doing to us? George Müeller, the famed nineteenth-century founder of orphanages that cared for thousands of children and handled millions of dollars donated on faith, said: "The beginning of anxiety is the end of faith. The beginning of true faith is the end of anxiety."[2]

Paul's Prescription for Worry

Paul would have liked Müeller's quote because it nicely

sums up something he wrote to the Philippians: "Don't worry over anything whatever; whenever you pray tell God every detail of your needs in thankful prayer, and the peace of God, which surpasses human understanding, will keep constant guard over your hearts and minds as they rest in Christ Jesus" (Phil. 4:6,7, *Phillips*).

Paul's solution to worry is prayer. It's a simple solution, but anyone who has tried it knows it can also be complex, even frustrating. What happens when you pray and your worries seem to increase?

To get the full meaning of verses 6 and 7, you have to go back to verses 4 and 5. The kind of prayer that keeps worry at bay is based on "rejoicing in the Lord" and being "gentle toward everyone."

The Greek word Paul uses for *gentleness* could also be translated as "kindliness, sweet reasonableness, charitableness, mildness or generosity," to name a few. Commentator William Hendriksen believes there is no single word in the English language that fully expresses the meaning of the original Greek. Hendriksen prefers the term *big heartedness,* because a Christian can't be truly happy—or free from anxiety—without striving to be a blessing to others.[3]

Paul also tucks in the thought, "the nearness of your Lord" (v. 5), which can be interpreted in two ways: (1) Christ is coming back soon; (2) Christ is always nearby or present in your life. Perhaps Paul meant it both ways. He spoke often of the second coming of Christ (see 1 Cor. 1:7, 1 Thes. 5:23, 1 Tim. 6:14, Tit. 2:13). He also emphasized Christ's presence in the life of the believer (see Gal. 2:20, Eph. 3:17-19, Col. 1:27).

Whatever Paul meant, he rejoiced in the Lord with trust and faith. And when you're in the Lord, you don't have to be anxious about anything. You can take every-

thing to God in prayer and then enjoy His peace.

Does it sound a little too simple? One reason we let worry rob us of peace is that we think too much and believe too little. As he opens his provocative book *A Hunger for Meaning,* Calvin Miller compares reason and faith and calls them "quarrelsome brothers." Reason is the cynic, accusing faith of emotionalism and empty-headedness. But faith is the optimist, inching its way forward ever so slowly, never giving up, always kind and hopeful.[4]

There will always be tension between reason and faith. But when the stress level rises, it would do us well to lean a little harder on faith than on our ability to reason with the cold, hard facts.

Facts pile up in our lives like cord wood and leave us with plenty to worry about: the house payment is due next week . . . we're facing a lay-off . . . a grandchild lies in the hospital with meningitis . . . a loved one was supposed to be home hours ago and has not called . . . an important deadline closes in and the job isn't even half finished, and the list goes on.

Many believers memorize Philippians 4:6,7, so they can repeat these verses in times of stress or trouble. But memorizing these verses may not be of much help if you look on them as spiritual Band-Aids to slap on the situation. As Philippians 4:4,5 teaches, the assurances of Philippians 4:6,7 are based on a life-style that is built on being in Christ, rejoicing in Him and being considerate and charitable because you feel His presence always.

What Paul seems to be telling us is to not hit the prayer button simply to avoid the panic button. Instead, you turn *everything* over to God *before* it happens, and Paul literally means *everything* and *before.*

The clever little slogan advises: Don't sweat the small

stuff. But we do sweat the small stuff and can easily build it into big stuff if we start dwelling on it. But in Christ, we can let God sweat *all stuff*, big or small.

Prayer should be the first resort, not the last. Instead of waiting for a major crisis and saying, "This is *really* serious—I'd better pray about it," it makes more sense to be serious with God in the minor and mundane things of life. That way, it's much easier to draw strength and peace from Him when things are really on the line.

What Can Hijackers Do to Me?

In June of 1985 the world watched in horror as TWA Flight 847 was held hostage on a Beirut runway for 17 days. The captain of the plane was John Testrake, who had been planning to celebrate his wedding anniversary with his wife a few days later.

During the first moments when he realized flight 847 was hijacked, Captain Testrake was so busy trying to land the plane at the Beirut airport that he had no time to think about much of anything. As he taxied down the Beirut runway, a hijacker held a cocked pistol against his head and a hand grenade with its pin pulled directly in front of his face, making it almost impossible to see. Testrake, a committed Christian, confesses that it was at this moment the thought first crossed his mind that everyone in the plane could be dead in the next five minutes.

But in the next few seconds, another thought entered his head: *Well, that wouldn't be so bad. Because if I die, I'll get to see Jesus!*

From that moment on, God's peace flooded Testrake's mind and soul. He asserts that he can honestly say he never experienced another moment of fear during the 17-day ordeal that followed. He did worry about the well-being of the passengers and how his wife was coping, but he was never afraid for his own safety.

"I knew that if God didn't want me to die, there was nothing that the hijackers could do to kill me," Testrake writes. "He would see to it that the grenade didn't go off or that the trigger didn't get pulled. If He did allow me to die—well, He knows best and everything goes according to His plan."

John Testrake had many opportunities to test his faith in the days that followed, but somehow he and most of the crew and passengers survived. He recalls, "Looking back on it now, I'm amazed. The typical human impulse would have been to go to pieces—but God was there in a real, tangible way and He kept me strong!"[5]

Or as Paul would put it, "And God's peace, which is far beyond human understanding, will keep your hearts and minds safe, in Christ Jesus" (Phil. 4:7, *TEV*).

How to "Outpersist" the Devil

One of the paradoxes of Scripture is that, while it often speaks of peace for the believer (see John 14:27, 16:33; Rom. 5:1), it also describes the never ending war to be fought against the world (see 2 Cor. 10:3-6), the flesh or human nature (see Rom. 7:23) and the devil (Eph. 6:10-12).

God gives us many weapons to fight this battle (see Eph. 6:13-17), but above all He says to stay "alert and persistent as you pray" (Eph. 6:18, *Phillips*). If we value the peace that passes understanding, we must value prayer even more, because Satan's always on the prowl and ready to attack. Peter advises us to beware of our enemy the devil who prowls about like a lion hunting prey (1 Pet. 5:8,9).

An old story tells of a lady who never spoke ill of anyone. A friend told her, "I believe you would say something good even about the devil."

"Well," she said, "you certainly do have to admire his persistence."[6]

And it's true; the devil never gives up, never stops working. In C. S. Lewis's classic, *Screwtape Letters*, Satan writes to his nephew, Wormwood, and reminds him that it's always best to keep the Christian from praying at all. At least try to keep him in a state of offering superficial prayers that are vague and meaningless. The point is to get the believer to not really think about God. As Screwtape says, "It is funny how mortals always picture us as putting things into their minds: in reality our best work is done by keeping things out."[7]

If the devil is persistent, then we must be more so. In fact, we must be *importunate*—willing to bring our requests to God again and again and again, asking for what we need, persistently and repeatedly.

Jesus told two parables to teach persistence in prayer, one about a man who went to his neighbor in the middle of the night to borrow food to feed an unexpected guest, and the other about a poor widow who kept badgering a cold-hearted judge for justice.

Both stories have an almost comic flavor, and it's not too hard to picture Jesus' eyes twinkle as He tells them. In the case of the needy neighbor, his reluctant friend almost sounds like Archie Bunker as he says he has nothing to give and, besides, he's in bed with his children and can't get up! But persistence pays off and the needy neighbor finally gets what he needs (see Luke 11:5-8).

In the story of the widow and the unjust judge (see 18:1-5), the beleaguered magistrate finally gives in to the determined lady "so that she won't eventually wear me

keep ON asking, even after MIDNIGHT

out with her coming" (v. 5). The widow must have been one tough customer. The Greek words translated "lest she wear me out" can also be translated "lest she give me a black eye"!

If Jesus hadn't made further comment, both parables would make God sound like a selfish, begrudging sort who finally answers prayer to get people off His back. In both cases, of course, Jesus is teaching exactly the opposite.

After telling the story of the neighbor who persistently asked for bread at midnight, Jesus urged His disciples to ask, seek and knock because God would answer, they would find, and the door would be opened (see 11:9,10). After all, Jesus pointed out, if parents who are evil—

WHeN We aSK iN
PRaYeR BeLieViNG,
We SHaLL FiNaLLY
Receive, BUT
NOT NeceSSaRiLY
aCCORDING TO
OUR TiMeTaBLe.

sinful—know how to give good gifts to their children, think of what your heavenly Father will give those who ask Him (see vv. 11-13).

And if an unjust judge finally comes through with a just ruling for a persistent widow, "will not God bring about justice for his chosen ones?" (see 18:7).

R. A. Torrey points out that the persistence shown by the neighbor and widow literally mean *shamelessness.* "God," says Torrey, "delights in the holy boldness that will not take *no* for an answer. It is an expression of great faith and nothing pleases God more than faith. We should be careful about what we ask from God. But, when we do begin to pray for a thing, we should never give up praying for it until we receive it or until God makes it very clear and very definite that it is not His will to give it."[8]

These two parables teach two sides of a great truth: (1) to be persistent and never stop praying; (2) to trust a generous and loving God to give us what we need. When we ask in prayer believing, we shall finally receive, but not necessarily according to our timetable.

God Is Sufficient—No Matter What

William Barclay observes that we should never expect to get everything we might pray for. Only God sees the entire picture and what is best for us in the long run. Barclay writes: "We will never grow weary in prayer, and our faith will never falter if, after we have offered to God *our* prayers and requests, we add the perfect prayer, *Thy* will be done."[9]

As Jesus said, we "should always pray and not give up" (Luke 18:1, *NIV*). This is exactly what Paul is saying in Philippians 4:6,7. Instead of letting worry and anxiety eat at us until we're ready to throw in the towel, we are to take all of our problems and needs to God, faithfully and persistently, always asking that His will be done, and thanking Him in advance for what He knows is best. The answers we desire may be delayed or may be denied, but the peace that passes all understanding can be ours immediately, if we can leave our concerns in God's hands instead of just wringing ours.

Once again we see that behind holding any Christian value is *the bedrock issue of how much we value God and trust Him*. To value prayer is to value, above all, the Lord to whom we pray, acknowledging that He is completely in charge.

In Philippians 4:6,7, Paul is not saying, "If you trust Christ, you'll never have any cares or worries." He is saying, "In your cares, don't fret and fume and worry. Trust Christ. Thank Him for His Lordship, then *relax*. He will take it from there."

That's not always easy, but it is possible if we can remember a few basic facts:

God loves us.

God is sovereign.

God is sufficient—*no matter what*.

Woody Hayes, the legendary coach of Ohio State for many years, often told the story of how he came to that giant university to coach football after gaining experience at small schools like Denison and Miami of Ohio. The first time Hayes stood in the middle of the empty OSU stadium he looked at those 86,000 seats and began having second thoughts. Woody's young son was holding his hand and must have sensed his father's anxiety over having to try to create teams that could perform successfully before so many fanatical Buckeye followers. With wisdom far beyond his years, the little boy said, "But, Daddy, the football field is the same size."[10]

As we play the game of life, it may help to remember that no matter how overwhelming things may look, or how inadequate we may feel, *the field is still the same size.* And, even more important, the one who made the field is on our side.

> Don't worry about anything; instead, pray about everything; tell God your needs and don't forget to thank him for his answers. If you do this, you will experience God's peace, which is far more wonderful than the human mind can understand. His peace will keep your thoughts and hearts quiet and at rest as you trust in Christ Jesus." (Phil. 4:6,7, *TLB*).

The following questions are designed for your personal study or to discuss with a group. Record your answers in your journal/notebook.

1. On a scale of 1 to 10, do you worry a little or a lot (10 being a lot)?

2. How do you feel when someone says it's a sin to worry? What does Paul actually say in Philippians 4:6,7?

3. Do you think "rejoicing in the Lord" and being "gentle toward everyone" can reduce worry? (see Phil. 4:4,5). Why or why not? Note all the different possible translations for the Greek word Paul uses for "gentleness." Do people you know who are kindly, reasonable, loving, mild and generous worry a lot? What kind of people do a lot of worrying?

4. Which interpretation of "the nearness of your Lord" (v. 5) appeals most to you? Which interpretation might help you do less worrying? Why?

5. Do you agree or disagree with the statement: "But when the stress level rises, it would do us well to lean a little harder on faith than on our ability to reason with the cold, hard facts"? What are some cold, hard facts that sometimes cause you worry and anxiety?

6. How can you keep Philippians 4:6,7 from being a spiritual Band-Aid? Which is true of you? Do you tend to ask God for help with: Big stuff; Small stuff; All stuff. Have you ever caught yourself saying: "This is really serious—I'd better pray about it"? What were the circumstances?

7. What kept Captain John Testrake going during the hijacking of Flight 847 by terrorists? How was he a living example of Philippians 4:7?

8. List some reasons why the Christian should stay alert and persistent in prayer (see Rom. 7:23; 2 Cor. 10:3-6; Eph. 6:10-12,18).

9. C. S. Lewis has Screwtape saying, "It is funny how

mortals always picture us as putting things into their minds: in reality our best work is done by keeping things out." What did C. S. Lewis mean when he had Satan make this observation?

10. What does Jesus teach you in His two parables of importunate —persistent—prayer? (see Luke 11:5-13 and 18:1-8). Read R. A. Torrey's quote in this chapter. Under what circumstances should we "give up" and stop praying?

11. Do you agree or disagree that the perfect prayer is "Thy will be done"? Why or why not?

12. Do you agree or disagree with the statement: The answers (to prayer) we desire may be delayed or may be denied, but the peace that passes all understanding can be ours immediately, if we can leave our concerns in God's hands instead of just wringing ours. Why is it hard to leave our concerns in God's hands?

Taking Stock and Setting Goals

1. I worry most about:

2. I take my cares and concerns to God: ＿＿ all the time; ＿＿ sometimes; ＿＿ seldom.

3. I experience God's peace in prayer: ＿＿ all the time; ＿＿ sometimes; ＿＿ seldom.

4. The prayer motto that fits me best is:

_____ The field is still the same size—and He made it.

_____ It's in God's hands, not mine.

_____ God is sufficient, no matter what.

5. I will persist in prayer concerning:

6. Concerns I plan to turn over to God right now are:

Lord, teach me to pray

I worry too much and pray too little. Help me remember to pray about *everything*—even the things I know I can handle. Somehow, Lord, get it through my head that you are in charge—and all I have to do is trust.

Notes
1. Quoted by Jerry A. Schmidt, *Do You Hear What You're Thinking?* (Wheaton, IL: Victor Books, 1983), p. 69.
2. Paul Lee Tan, *Encyclopedia of 7700 Illustrations* (Garland, TX: Assurance Publishers, 1979).
3. William Hendriksen, *New Testament Commentary, Exposition of Philippians* (Grand Rapids, MI: Baker Book House, 1962), p. 193.
4. Calvin Miller, *A Hunger for Meaning* (Downers Grove, IL: InterVarsity Press, 1984), p. 9.
5. John Testrake with Dave J. Wimbish, *Triumph over Terror on Flight 847* (Old Tappan, NJ: Fleming H. Revell Co., 1987), p. 75.
6. Tan, *Illustrations*, p. 1235.
7. C. S. Lewis, *Screwtape Letters* (Chicago: Lord and King Associates, Inc., 1976), p. 34.
8. R. A. Torrey, *How to Pray* (Springdale, PA: Whitaker House, 1983), pp. 50,51.
9. William Barclay, *The Gospel of Luke, Daily Study Bible* (Edinburgh: The St. Andrew Press, 1953), p. 231.
10. Tan, *Illustrations*, p. 1649.

CHAPTER NINE

THE SOUNDNESS OF SERIOUS THINKING

*T*here is an old saying that claims 5 percent of people think, 15 percent think they think, and 80 percent would rather die than think. These sardonic words are more amusing than accurate, because we all think hundreds and even thousands of thoughts every day.

William Barclay observes that the human mind will always set itself upon something. If Christians should value anything, it is setting their minds on the right kinds of thoughts. [1]

The question is, "What thoughts are the right kind and how can I learn to think them consistently?"

In recent years, dozens of books, tape albums and seminars have sought to tell us how to think. One of the most popular approaches is "positive thinking" which became well-known through Dr. Norman Vincent Peale's best- seller *The Power of Positive Thinking.*

Dr. Peale based his positive-thinking philosophy on the teachings of Jesus Christ, but since he coined the term, many others have used it as a label for quick fix formulas to gain riches, fame, success or power. Many people have claimed positive thinking has changed their lives, turned business disasters into successes, saved their failing marriages and even cured their gout.

Others, however, aren't so sure. They say that positive thinking is simply a cop-out to cover up fear or a lack of confidence. Trying to talk yourself into a positive attitude is like trying to smother a fire with a cardboard box. You may succeed momentarily, but eventually the flames of stress and tension will flare up even higher.[2]

Why does positive thinking seem to work for some but not for others? How should the Christian use it, if at all? What would the apostle Paul advise? Ironically, Paul is often called one of the original positive thinkers because of Philippians 4:8:

> Finally, brothers, whatever is true, whatever is noble, whatever is right, whatever is pure, whatever is lovely, whatever is admirable—if anything is excellent or praiseworthy—think about such things.

While many of the things Paul mentions sound positive, he actually has another approach in mind. The word he uses for *think* means to "take under thoughtful consideration or carefully reflect upon."[3] In other words, Paul advises us to do serious thinking that centers on Jesus Christ and God's peace (look back at vv. 6, 7).

Unfortunately, as Paul himself learned, you can know Christ and still slip back into wrong thinking (see Paul's struggles with sinful thoughts in Rom. 7:15-23). He often reminded believers to emphasize "the mind of Christ" (1 Cor. 2:16), and to set their minds on things above instead of things on earth (see Col. 3:2). Instead of being tied up with bills, plans, projects and schedules, we are to do holy thinking that centers on what is infinite and eternal.

This is difficult. We fear becoming so heavenly minded we will be no earthly good. Actually, there is little danger of that. What we need to think about is becoming heavenly minded enough to let God use us to do more good on earth.

But you don't become heavenly minded by gritting your teeth every morning and saying, "I'm going to think

WHEN QUESTIONABLE THOUGHTS COME,
ask FOR THE PASSWORD.

holy, serious thoughts today if it kills me." Nor is it necessary to ignore the bills or other realities of life.

The first step toward holy, serious thinking is to "gird
up the loins" of your mind—that is, prepare your mind for
action by being self-controlled (see 1 Pet. 1:13).

The self-controlled Christian is self-disciplined, or as
Paul puts it: "firm, incapable of being moved" (1 Cor.
15:58, *Williams*). Self-control and self-discipline are keys
to having holy and heavenly thoughts.

The next obvious question is how do we discipline our
thoughts? In *Control Yourself!* author Del Kehl suggests
that Christians picture the mind as a renovated palace that
can be assailed by a hideous throng of evil things—ugly

thoughts. But when God's peace stands guard at the door of your mind, ugly thoughts are stymied.

The sentinel cries, "Halt, in the name of the monarch who controls this citadel! What are your credentials? What is the password?" If the thought, attitude or mind-set lacks the proper credentials and doesn't know the password, it cannot get in.[4]

When perverse or even useless thoughts come knocking at the door of your mind, don't simply say, "Why, come on in and let's talk." Instead, ask for the password. Better yet, ask for any number of passwords that Paul catalogues in Philippians 4:8, which contains eight sub-values strung together much like pearls in a necklace. Sound, serious, *spiritually positive* thinking always asks:

Is it *true?*

Is it *honest?*

Is it *right?*

Is it *pure?*

Is it *lovely?*

Is it *admirable?*

Is it *excellent?*

Is it *praiseworthy?*

The Best Illustration of Philippians 4:8

At several points we have centered on the concept that

behind every Christian value stands the Supreme Value of all—Jesus Christ. The best illustration of all of the eight virtue/values in Philippians 4:8 is Jesus Himself.

Jesus was the perfect expression of what is true. He said as much to His confused and doubting disciples on the night before the Crucifixion: "I am the way and the truth and the life" (John 14:6). Pilate was looking truth right in the eye but didn't seem to know it when he asked Jesus, "What is truth?" (18:38).

Jesus' life and words stood for what is reliable and real. He always mercilessly uncovered and exposed the false, the unreal, the phony or the plastic. Telling the truth is not always easy. Sometimes it can be difficult, sticky or even dangerous. But in the long run it is always worthwhile.

The aged father of the great philosopher, Emmanuel Kant, was making a perilous journey through the forests of Poland when he was held up by robbers who demanded everything he had.

"Have you given us all?" they asked as they made ready to go with his purse, prayer book and horse.

"All," said the old man, trembling, but when he was safely out of their sight, his hand touched something hard in the hem of his robe. It was gold, sewn there for safety and totally forgotten in fear during the robbery. At this point you would expect old Mr. Kant to hurry on his way rejoicing, but instead he went back to find the robbers!

"I've told you what was not true," he said, "it was unintentional. I was too terrified to think. Here, take the gold in my robes." There was dead silence. Then to the old man's amazement, one robber came forward and handed back his purse. Another restored his book of prayer, while another brought him his horse and helped him mount. Then, after asking him to bless them, the robbers watched the old man slowly ride away.[5]

We can call the old gentleman naive, even foolish, but the story forces us to ask the question: "How much do I value truth and what risks am I willing to take to tell it?"

Jesus was the epitome of what is noble and honest. The Greek word Paul uses here refers to what the Greeks characteristically used to describe their gods, what they felt was worthy of reverence. Jesus is the ultimate object of the Christian's reverence and worship. He calls us away from the flaky and frivolous and bids us daily to follow Him to find what is honorable, serious, rightly motivated—those things with the dignity of holiness upon them. Words like *true, noble* and *honest* all suggest the value covered in chapter 5—integrity.

Frank Gaebelein founded the famed Stony Brook School in New York and was also a co-editor of *Christianity Today.* His daughter, Gretchen Gaebelein Hull, remembers that she, her sister and brother, watched their father as he sought to be obedient to God and make his private life consistent with his public image. He easily spotted phonies and didn't want anything phony about his own life.

In an article written for the magazine of which her father was co-editor, Gretchen paid him this tribute: "Long before I knew how to spell the word, or even knew what it meant, I realized my father was a man of integrity. Later I would learn phrases like 'Christian commitment' and 'devotion to duty,' but from my earliest years I simply knew that Frank Gaebelein 'rang true.'"[6]

There is no better example of what is right or just than Jesus Himself. The word *integrity* has to do with duty—a sense of responsibility, facing your duty and getting it done. No one did his duty with more eagerness and discipline than Jesus. As a young boy He told Joseph and Mary that He had to be about His Father's business (see Luke 2:49). When criticized for breaking Sabbath laws, He told the Jews that He sought not to please Himself but the one who sent Him (see John 5:30).

The worldly system invites us to lose ourselves in seeking pleasure, goofing off and getting by with as little work as possible. We are taught to ask, "What's in it for me?" or to justify just about anything by saying, "I've got to meet my needs." Jesus teaches us to ask, "What's in it for God" and "How can I do my duty to Him and my fellow-man?"

Jesus is ultimate purity. Compared to Christ, the best men and women are defiled, dirty and sordid. David was called a man after God's own heart, yet he committed adultery with Bathsheba and wound up having her husband murdered to cover his tracks (see 2 Sam. 11).

We may think we are clever enough to leave no tracks that others can find, but we always have thoughts that God can read. How then can we fight what seems a hopeless battle for purity? First, when our thoughts are not clean enough to stand God's scrutiny, we must gratefully use the promise of 1 John 1:9, which guarantees we can be cleansed of impurity by confessing our sins. Second, we are not to use 1 John 1:9 to buy cheap grace. Because we cannot live perfect lives is no reason to wallow in immorality and impurity. In Paul's words to the Roman Christians, "God forbid!" (Rom. 6:2, *KJV*).

Television has been called a vast wasteland, but today it has also become a vast cesspool. So are a large number of films, books and magazines. Being pure doesn't necessarily mean being limited to the Disney channel, but what does it mean? It is all too easy to sacrifice purity on the altar of sophisticated adult entertainment. A lot of so-called adult entertainment is nothing more than rationalizing lust and immorality by calling it art, beauty or real life.

In October 1987, Jessica Hahn appeared on the Phil

Donahue Show to explain to his studio audience and millions of TV viewers why she posed half-nude for *Playboy* magazine. Defiant and hostile, she became hotly indignant when many in the audience questioned her credibility for taking an estimated 1 million dollars for letting *Playboy* run the pictures.

Jessica let the audience and viewers know that she had sul_ red terribly at the hands of evangelist Jim Bakker and she dared anyone to "walk in her shoes" for even a few days. Her arguments included the observations that: "What God made is good and should be appreciated . . . I have greater faith in God than ever . . . God wants me to be happy." Totally lacking was any mention of repentance, regret, or that God might want her to be pure, holy or at least wise enough not to be a stumbling block and to avoid the appearance of evil.

It's easy, of course, to criticize Jessica Hahn for hypocrisy and fuzzy thinking, but it is more useful to ask, "What of *my* values? What would I do if offered a million dollars to do something 'questionable'? More to the point, what do I do with questionable choices each day when offered much less?"

Jesus was also the supreme example of what is lovely, or winsome. The word Paul uses here means "that which calls forth love." Things that are lovely are not necessarily easily described in scientific or quantitative terms. In our high-tech world of computers, we can miss what is lovely in favor of what we think is accurate, efficient or precise.

Well-known columnist James J. Kilpatrick bought a computer program that not only could scan his copy for errors, but could also tell him about grammar, usage, style and punctuation. In short, the computer could tell Kilpatrick the difference between good writing and bad. Just for fun he fed it some of his own copy and the machine promptly told him he was a lousy writer.

Then Kilpatrick tried Lincoln's Gettysburg Address. The computer informed him that Abe's writing style was very weak because he was wordy and used too much of the passive voice. It also observed that Lincoln used too many adjectives, that most of his sentences contained multiple clauses and that he should try to write more simply.[7]

So much for a computer's analysis of one of the most inspiring pieces of prose ever penned. Today the Gettysburg Address is still seen as a lovely piece of work, done by a man who understood his nation's hopes, fears and pain. Efficient and precise thoughts are good; lovely ones nurture the soul.

Jesus was also the ultimate example of what is admirable or gracious. The *King James Version* says, "good report" (Phil. 4:8). The Greek word literally means "fair speaking" and the Greeks often used it in reference to the holy silence at the beginning of a sacrifice in the presence of the gods. William Barclay observes that this word "describes the things which are fit for God to hear."[8]

Even when He spoke in sharp reproof, Jesus never used ugly or ungracious words. If we think on things that are admirable, we are less likely to fall into the vicious cycle that sees us responding to an angry or biting word with something angry and biting ourselves. When we think about being gracious and helpful, we will not shoot from the hip with phrases like:

How many times do I have to tell you?

What's the matter with you? Don't you remember what we decided?

WHEN YOU
THROW MUD
YOU ALWAYS
LOSE GROUND.

> I can't help it if you're upset—that's your problem.

The next time these and other retorts leap to your lips, think of some admirable words from Jesus Himself: "Love your enemies, do good to those who hate you, bless those who curse you, pray for those who mistreat you" (Luke 6:27,28, *NASB*).

When the heat is on, it's much easier to go for the clever retort. The ancient Jews took a backseat to no one when it came to cutting put-downs. One of their favorites was: "May every tooth in your head fall out but one, and may it have a cavity." Mudslinging is the oldest game in the world, but when you throw mud you always lose ground.[9]

Jesus was the summum bonum *of excellence.* He never wrote a book like *The Pursuit of Excellence*; He simply pursued excellence every moment of His earthly ministry. As we follow Him we are called to seek what is virtuous and lofty and to shun what is shoddy, inferior and done with the attitude of just trying to get by.

Finally, no one is more praiseworthy than Jesus. He also taught us something about how to use praise and encouragement. He tore down hypocrisy that did not honor God but always reached out a hand to help and encourage sinners.

Thinking praise-centered thoughts may be one of our most difficult tasks. Not only do we live in a sordid world where so much is not deserving of praise, but we have a natural inclination to be critical and judgmental. It is easy to think about what is wrong with our church, our pastor, our spouse, our children. It is more difficult to give thought to what's right with the people and institutions in our lives.

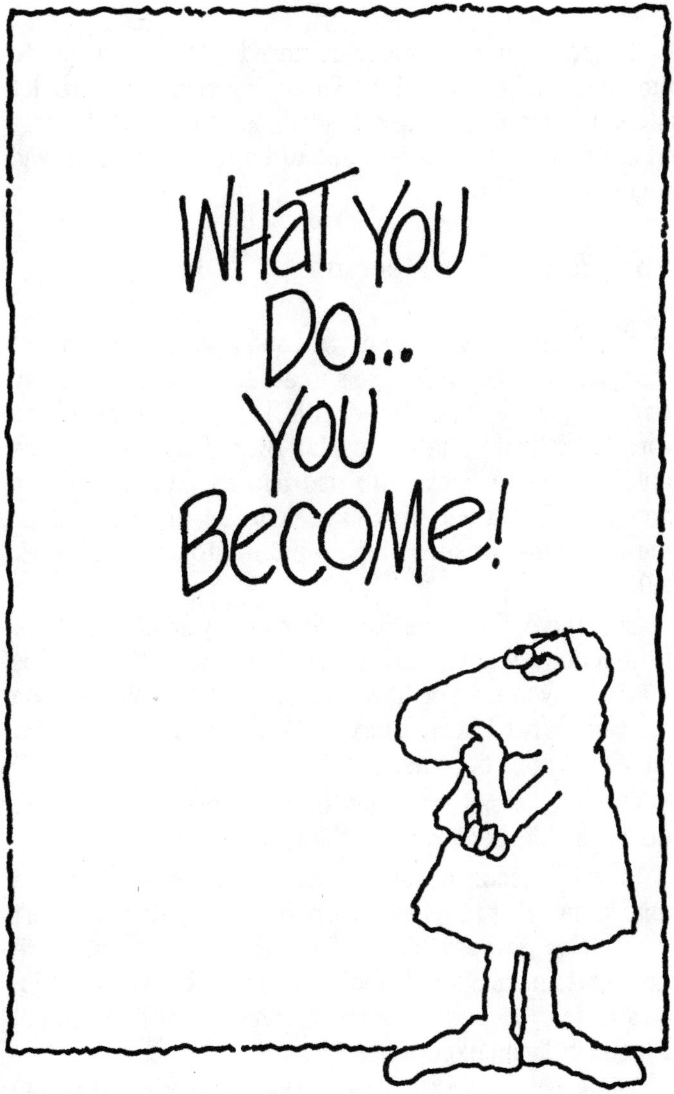
WHAT YOU DO... YOU BECOME!

To stay on the praise-centered path, it helps to remember Hebrews 13:15: "Through Jesus, therefore, let us continually offer to God a sacrifice of praise." A heart full of praise to God is less apt to be full of criticism and judgment of others.

What You Do You Become

Another truth we have seen again and again in our study of Philippians is that values are something we do, not simply something we recite or agree with. Paul not only heard the Word and taught it; he was such a *doer of the Word* that he could tell the Philippians to use him as their model and example! "Whatever you have learned or received or heard from me, or seen in me—put it into practice" (Phil. 4:9).

In verse 9, Paul gives the complete cycle of education. He mentions *hearing* and *seeing*, but the bottom line is *doing* what you say you have learned. It was a wise person who said: What I hear, I forget. What I see, I remember. But what I do, I become. [10]

Or as Jesus put it, "Now that you know these things, you will be blessed if you do them" (John 13:17).

Stuart Briscoe observes that if we don't learn, we won't know what to do and the result will be that we won't do much or be very blessed. On the other hand, if we know certain things but don't do them, we will, in Briscoe's terms, become "dismal archives of truth instead of galleries of living experience."

The secret, says Briscoe, is this: "If you do what you know, and what you know is the result of meditation and the truth of God . . . you will be blessed and be a blessing." [11]

LIFeTOUCH DePARTMeNT

The following questions are designed for your personal study or to discuss with a group. Record your answers in your journal/notebook.

1. Why is it so important for Christians to set their minds on the right kinds of thoughts? Does the Church put enough emphasis on the Christian's thought life or is there too much emphasis on outward appearance and performance?

2. Why has positive thinking become so popular? Why does it work for some but not others? Has it worked for you? Under what circumstances?

3. Review the definition of *think* in this chapter. How would you differentiate between serious spiritual thinking and positive thinking?

4. What thoughts does the term *heavenly minded* bring to your mind?
   ____ Ethereal   ____ Super spiritual
   ____ Impractical   ___ Other: _____

   How could someone become so heavenly minded he or she would be of no earthly good?

5. When perverse, evil or useless thoughts come knocking at the door of your mind, how do you handle them? Can Philippians 4:8 really help? How?

6. What do the following passages tell you about how a Christian should think and how to keep out the wrong kind of thoughts? See Proverbs 23:7, especially the *The New King James Version* or *New American Standard Bible* (see also Isa. 26:3; Rom. 12:1,2; Eph. 4:19-23; 1 Pet. 4:7).

7. How can Colossians 3:16 help you discipline your thoughts? Name three ways you are letting the Word of Christ dwell in you richly.

8. According to this chapter, sound, serious "spiritually positive" thinking always asks eight questions. Which of these questions do you ask most? Which do you ask least?

9. Many things can be "true" but what kind of truth does the Christian seek? (see Prov. 23:23; Zech. 8:16,17; John 1:14, 14:6, 18:37,38; Eph. 4:15,25). Is it possible to use truth in a selfish, harmful way?

10. Write a brief description of "an honest person." Compare your description with the story of Emmanuel Kant's father and the robbers, as well as Gretchen Hull's tribute to her father, Frank Gaebelein. In your opinion, are most Christians truly honest? Should they be? Why or why not?

11. If what is right or just has to do with duty, what are the Christian's duties? (see Ps. 61:8; Prov. 8:34; Luke 9:23—daily duties; John 13:35; 1 Pet. 1:22; 1 John 4:7—duties to Christian brothers and sisters; Mark 12:31; Rom. 15:2—duties to neighbors; Matt.

25:35—duties to the needy and the stranger; Acts 20:35; Rom. 14:1—duties to the weak).

12. Was any man or woman in Scripture (besides Jesus) completely pure? What of David who was a man after God's own heart? What does Scripture tell us about pursuing purity? (see Ps. 24:3,4; Matt. 5:8; Eph. 4:17-24; Col. 3:5; 1 Tim. 1:5; Jas. 1:27; 1 Pet. 1:22; 2 Pet. 3:14).

13. What would you say to Jessica Hahn if she told you she posed for *Playboy* and took 1 million dollars because she "knew God wanted her to be happy"? How could you share with her God's desire for the Christian to be pure (see 1 John 3:2,3), holy (see 2 Cor. 7:1), to not be a stumbling block (see Rom. 14:12,13) and to avoid the appearance of evil in any form? (see 1 Thess. 5:22). What about your own purity? How would you answer the question: What would you do if someone offered you a million dollars to do something questionable? What if it were only *slightly* questionable?

14. Review the section on the word *lovely*. Why is something lovely hard to describe in scientific or quantitative terms? What program or film have you seen recently that would fit the description of lovely?

15. The definition in this chapter of "admirable or gracious" includes the kinds of thoughts that are fit for God to hear. Why do we all too often use ungracious, biting, cutting words instead of those that are admirable and gracious? What forces are at work? How can you counter these forces?

16. What does Philippians 4:9 have to do with being a Christian from the inside out? Which is most important: hearing, seeing or doing? Why? (see Matt. 7:21, 12:50; John 13:17; Rom. 2:13; Jas. 1:22).

17. Do you agree or disagree: If we know certain things but don't do them, we will become "dismal archives of truth instead of galleries of living experience." Describe a Christian who is a dismal archive of truth. How could he or she turn into a gallery of living experience?

Taking Stock and Setting Goals

1. My thought life is:

1	2	3	4	5	6	7	8	9	10

Unsound   Sound
Impure   Pure
Muddled   Clear

2. Questions I need to ask more often are:
   _____ Is it true or is it rumor?
   _____ Is it honest or is it flaky?
   _____ Is it right or is it a cop-out?
   _____ Is it pure and wholesome or is it questionable, sordid, dirty?
   _____ Is it lovely and winsome or is it off-color, ugly?
   _____ Is it honorable and gracious or is it irritable, demeaning or cutting?
   _____ Is it excellent or is it second-class, shoddy?
   _____ Is it praiseworthy or is it destructive, critical?

3. My personal goals for disciplining my thoughts are:

Lord, guard my thinking

Help me gird up the loins of my mind; give me the self-control to take bad thoughts captive and turn them into obedience to you. Make me aware that I choose my thoughts. Help me choose those that please you.

Notes
1. William Barclay, *The Letter to the Philippians, Colossians, Thessalonians, The Daily Study Bible* (Edinburgh: The St. Andrew Press, 1959), pp. 103,104.
2. Robert Kreigel and Marilyn Harris Kreigel, *The C Zone: Peak Performance Under Pressure* (New York: Fawcett, Div. of Random House, 1985).
3. W. E. Vine, *Vine's Expository Dictionary of Old and New Testament Words* (Old Tappan, NJ: Fleming H. Revell Co., 1981), p. 127, para. 5 (logizomai).
4. Del Kehl, *Control Yourself!* (Grand Rapids, MI: Zondervan Publishing House, 1982), p. 103.
5. Paul Lee Tan, *Encyclopedia of 7700 Illustrations* (Garland, TX: Assurance Publishers, 1979), p. 1529.
6. Gretchen Gaebelein Hull, "Frank Gaebelein: Character Before Career," *Christianity Today*, Sept. 21, 1984, pp. 14-18. Cited by Joseph A. Ryan, "Wanted: People of Integrity," *Discipleship Journal*, Issue 31, 1985, p. 20.
7. John R. Noe, *People Power* (Nashville, TN: Oliver-Nelson, Div. of Thomas Nelson Publishers, 1986), p. 128.
8. Barclay, *Letter to the Philippians.*
9. Quoted by Ken Durham, *Speaking from the Heart* (Fort Worth, TX: Sweet Publishing Co., 1986), p. 71.
10. Noe, *People Power*, p. 137.
11. Stuart Briscoe, *Bound for Joy* (Ventura, CA: Regal Books, 1975), p. 154.

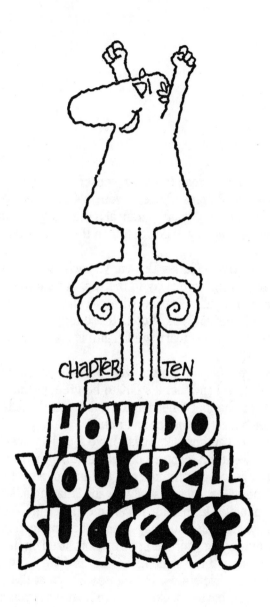

CHAPTER TEN

HOW DO YOU SPELL SUCCESS?

What does it mean to be a success?

If you're Robert Ringer, you believe success is wrapped up in doing your "personal moral duty" to pursue pleasure, as long as you don't step on the toes or rights of others.[1]

If you're Helen Gurley Brown, you achieve success by "mouseburgering" your way to the top, carefully blending hard work and self-discipline with calculated use of diet, exercise, clothes and sex. Put all those together correctly and love and a happy marriage fall into line as you wind up "having it all."[2]

If you're Michael Korda, you believe you have the right to succeed and that it's OK to be greedy, ambitious, look-out-for-Number-One, have a good time, be Machiavellian, dishonest, a winner and rich.[3]

Books and authors like these have found a ready audience in a twentieth- century society that is predominantly interested in self-gratification and self-improvement.

In America, success usually means "making it"—as in lots of money. Or making it can mean getting famous. Preferably, making it usually means becoming rich *and* famous and having your life-style immortalized on the television program of the same name. Or, making it can mean social or academic status, having heads turn at the sound of your voice, having necks crane to hear what you might think or say.

In *Being the Best*, behavioral psychologist and motivational specialist, Denis Waitley, warns that today success does not seem to depend any longer on holding traditional values like truth, morality and integrity. All these *old-fashioned* ideas have been shouldered aside by a brash new value system that feeds on success myths like:

If you've got it, flaunt it.

Go for the jugular, winning is what counts.

Winning isn't everything, it's the only thing!

Nice guys finish last.

Waitley's goal in *Being the Best* is to expose myths like those above, which he believes are enslaving us as a nation as well as individually. He observes, "Success is a very personal thing . . . . It is not what you *get* that makes you successful, it is *what you are continuing to do with what you've got.*"[4]

The self-help success myths never satisfy because success is not a destination like "the top" or "Number One." Success is a way of traveling. As one graduate of a Waitley seminar put it, "The road to success is always under construction."

And driving that road means obeying the traffic laws. A Manhattan real estate broker admitted: "I could have made a lot more money in my life, but I preferred to sleep well at night."[5]

How Did Paul Spell Success?

A poem by Ralph Waldo Emerson measures success this way:

> To laugh often and love much;
> To win the respect of intelligent people
>   And the affection of children;
> To earn the approbation of honest critics
>   And endure the betrayal of false friends;
> To appreciate beauty;
> To find the best in others;
> To give one's self;
> To leave the world a bit better,
>   Whether by a healthy child, a garden
>   patch, or
>   A redeemed social condition;
> To have played and laughed with enthusiasm
> and sung with exultation;
> To know even one other life has breathed easier
> Because you have lived—
> This is to have succeeded.[6]

Although the apostle Paul would have had his theological differences with a transcendentalist like Emerson, he would have liked his poem, for as far as it goes. Paul valued winning the respect and affection of others, he valued the appreciation of honest critics and he learned to endure the betrayal of false friends. He appreciated beauty and finding the best in others. He certainly left the world a bit better and many other lives breathed easier because he had lived. But Paul took all this one giant step farther. He valued success, *but only on God's terms*. He wanted to succeed, but only for God's glory, not his.

As Paul closes his letter to the Philippians, three final thoughts sum up his personal philosophy of success:

I have learned the secret of being content in any

Value Success
BUT ONLY
ON GOD'S
TERMS.

and every situation, whether well fed or hungry, whether living in plenty or in want" (Phil. 4:12).

I can do everything through him who gives me strength (v. 13).

And my God will meet all your needs according to his glorious riches in Christ Jesus (v. 19).

Why Pursuing Happiness Doesn't Work

When people think of success, they often think of happiness as well. In fact, many think real success is "being happy." Millions of people chase happiness every day. Harold Kushner, author of the best-selling *When Bad Things Happen to Good People*, observes that the Declaration of Independence guarantees all American citizens "life, liberty and the pursuit of happiness," but a political document can't warn us of the frustrations of trying to exercise our "rights."

Kushner believes the pursuit of happiness is the wrong goal. "You don't become happy by pursuing happiness. You become happy by living a life that means something."[7]

Kushner sees happiness as a by-product but never the primary goal. He believes happiness is like a butterfly. Chase it and it will fly away from you and hide, but stop chasing the butterfly and get busy doing productive, useful things and happiness "will sneak up on you from behind and perch on your shoulder."[8]

Paul, of course, never pursued happiness. He pursued Christ, always pressing toward the mark to become what Christ had asked him to be (see Phil. 3:12-16). Paul doesn't talk about happiness but he talks a great deal about

PURSUING HAPPINESS IS LIKE CHASING BUTTERFLIES.

joy, which might be called "happiness come of age."

Happiness depends on circumstances. When things go well, Happiness reigns supreme. When they go badly, Happiness rolls on the floor and has a temper tantrum.

Joy, on the other hand, overlooks or overrules circumstances. When things go well, Joy says "Rejoice—praise God!" When they go badly, Joy steadfastly says, "Rejoice anyhow!"

According to the New Testament, experiencing sorrow often paves the way for joy. Jesus said, "You will grieve, but your grief will turn to joy" (John 16:20). Paul told the Romans "we also rejoice in our sufferings, because we know that suffering produces perseverance; perseverance, character; and character, hope" (Rom 5:3,4).

James had the same idea when he opened his letter to Jewish Christians scattered everywhere by saying, "Consider it pure joy, my brothers, whenever you face trials of many kinds, because you know that the testing of your faith develops perseverance" (Jas. 1:2,3).

Jesus taught the listeners to His Sermon on the Mount that being persecuted for His sake would bring joy (see Matt. 5:11,12). James and John put that teaching into practice when the Sanhedrin scourged them for preaching about Jesus and they left "rejoicing because they had been counted worthy of suffering disgrace for the Name" (Acts 5:41).

Can all this rejoicing in the face of trials and persecution really happen? Are Christians supposed to be masochists? Insults, blows and tongue lashings hurt the Christian just as much as anyone else, but in all of Scripture the believer has joy because of God Himself. The psalmist calls God his joy and delight (see Ps. 43:4), and so does Paul, who says, "we also rejoice in God through our Lord Jesus Christ" (Rom. 5:11), "Finally, my brothers, rejoice in the Lord!" (Phil. 3:1), "Rejoice in the Lord always, I will say it again: rejoice!" (4:4).[9]

The Simple Secret of Contentment

Beginning in Philippians 4:10 Paul gets back to the main purpose of his letter: to pen a thank-you note to all his friends for all their help to him in his times of need. He knows they've been concerned about him but have had no opportunity to show it because they didn't even know where he was. Now that they have shown concern, he wants to thank them, but to also be sure they understand that his needs aren't the real point.

The true value in the gifts sent by the Philippians is that they are a "fragrant offering, an acceptable sacrifice, pleasing to God" (v.18). Their act of love has been credited to their heavenly account and this is what really matters.

Paul appreciates the gifts but he has learned what it is to be in need and what it is to have plenty. "I have learned the secret of being content in any and every situation, whether well fed or hungry, whether living in plenty or in want" (v.12).

If Paul had stopped here, he would have sounded like the Stoic philosophers of his day. In fact, in the Greek text he uses one of the great words of pagan ethics when he says he has learned to be *autarkes*, which means "entirely self-sufficient." This is what the Stoics believed and set as their highest goal in life. They wanted to reach a state of mind in which they were totally independent of all things and all people. The Stoic wanted to reach the point where he needed nothing or no one.[10]

Paul was no Stoic. He felt a sufficiency but only because God had come into his life. Paul was God-sufficient and that's what he means when he utters the famous line that has been memorized by millions of Christians: "I can do all things through Christ who strengthens me" (Phil. 4:13, *NKJV*).

When Paul uses the phrase *I can do all things*, he is in danger of being misunderstood, particularly if this verse is pulled out of context. But Paul isn't saying he is all-powerful and can do anything he wants. Paul knows that whatever the circumstances may be, he can do what needs to be done *within those circumstances. The Living Bible* paraphrase of Philippians 4:13 puts it well: "For I can do everything God asks me to with the help of Christ who gives me the strength and power."

In prison and facing death, Paul could say, "At the moment I have all I need—more than I need!" (v. 18, *TLB*). He goes on to assure the Philippians that God will also supply all their needs "from his riches in glory, because of what Christ Jesus has done for us" (v.19, *TLB*).

Summing Up the Meaning of Success

The following chart compares the meaning of success from the world's point of view and the values taught in Scripture. The world says, "Have it all;" the Bible tells us, "Give your all." The world says, "Look out for Number One;" the Bible says, "Look out for others." The world says, "Play to win and don't moralize;" the Bible says, "Play to lose your self-centeredness and hate immorality."

Success Is Not . . .	Success Is . . .
. . . a destination or goal you reach if you're strong enough, smart enough, clever enough.	. . . a way of traveling— your walk with God
. . . getting rich or making it through prestige, power, or possessions.	. . . bearing the fruit of the Spirit and developing a Christ-like attitude.
. . . climbing ever higher, whirling ever faster, burning out instead of rusting out.	. . . knowing when enough is enough, always ready to serve but at God's pace, not yours.

. . . being omnipotent, self-sufficient, totally capable.

. . . doing all things that are needed in a situation through Christ's strength, which is made perfect in your weakness (see 2 Cor. 12:9).

. . . feeling that you are inexpendable—if you want something done right, you have to do it yourself.

. . . knowing you are part of God's plan but never the whole show.

. . . Type A, 100-miles-per-hour behavior, is always seeking new heights of achievement— always pushing beyond established limits.

. . . knowing your limits, working up to capacity, seeking excellence but never at the price of being exhausted burned out.

. . . your highest value, what you must have at any price.

. . . a by-product of being obedient, serving and walking with God, always acknowledging Him as Creator, Savior and Lord.

The world's value system places highest regard on winning, being the best, making the most, going the farthest. Does that mean the Bible says all Christians must settle for mediocrity, second-best and some state of being losers in order to be gentle Christians, meek and mild? The record shows that many Christians have risen to the top of their profession or field. Their primary motivation, however, was not to glorify themselves, but to glorify God.

Do You Run to Feel His Pleasure?

Chapter 3 told the story of Eric Liddle, champion Olympic runner who later went to the mission field to serve as a relatively unknown teacher in the back country of China. Liddle proved he was one of the best in the 1924 Olympics when he won a Gold Medal in the 400-meter dash, after refusing to compete in the 100-meter dash, which was run on a Sunday. But he didn't train and compete with the goal of having his name immortalized in the history of track and field. Eric Liddle had a saying: "Every time I run I feel His pleasure." He ran because he loved to run and he knew that God approved.

Eric Liddle's motto is a good one for any follower of Christ. Whatever you do—wherever you run—do you feel God's pleasure?

Paul did. He would have liked Eric Liddle's saying and he said much the same thing in a letter to Timothy: "I have fought the good fight, I have finished the race, I have kept the faith. Now there is in store for me the crown of righteousness, which the Lord, the righteous Judge, will award to me on that day" (2 Tim. 4:7,8).

Paul became one of the world's great theologians and scholars, he became the writer of over half the New Testament, he became the major force who spread the gospel throughout the known world of the first century. Paul was a success but spelled it, C-H-R-I-S-T.

Whatever happened, in chains or out, hungry or well-fed, at the bottom of the barrel or the top of the heap, Paul was happy because he had all he needed in Jesus. To Emerson—and all the world—Paul says:

> To be content in any situation;
> To have strength to do all that is necessary;

To trust a God who supplies all I need—
This is to have succeeded!

The following questions are designed for your personal study or to discuss with a group. Record your answers in your journal/notebook.

1. Write down your personal definition of success. Compare it to the definitions in this chapter.

2. Why do current definitions of success, particularly on the secular scene, seem to ignore, or at least down play, traditional values like truth, morality and integrity?

3. Do you agree or disagree with the graduate of a Denis Waitley seminar who said, "The road to success is always under construction"? Why or why not?

4. Reread Ralph Waldo Emerson's poem. Is there anything in the poem that violates Christian values? What does the poem lack in regard to Christian values?

5. What was Paul's secret of contentment? (see Phil. 4:12). How did Paul learn this secret? (see 1 Cor. 4:8-13; 2 Cor. 11:24-33).

6. What was Paul's secret of strength and power? (see Phil. 4:13, compare 2 Cor. 12:1-10).

7. What was Paul's secret of abundance? (see Phil. 4:19 and compare with Prov. 10:22; John 10:10; 2 Cor. 9:8; Eph. 1:18, 3:8).

8. According to Harold Kushner's remarks in this chapter, why is it so futile to "pursue happiness"? How does he believe you become "happy"? Would Paul agree?

9. Complete these sentences:
Happiness depends on _____ .
Joy depends on _____ .

10. According to Philippians 4:10-18, for what is Paul thanking and praising the Philippians? Is it their gifts or is it something else?

11. In what sense does Paul sound like a Stoic in Philippians 4:12? How does Paul go beyond stoicism?

12. Eric Liddle, the Olympic Gold Medal winner who became a missionary, often said: "Every time I run I feel His pleasure." Whatever you do—wherever you run—do you feel His pleasure? Think of some examples.

Taking Stock and Setting Goals

1. Review the comparison of the world's view of success and the values taught in Scripture in the chart provided in this chapter. Which of these comparisons apply most directly to you? Why? For example, do you often feel you are inexpendable and that if you want something done right you have to do it yourself? If so, you should

remember that you are only *part* of God's plan, but never the whole show.

2. Go back to the Introduction and retake the Spiritual Values Inventory. Have you made any significant changes in the 10 value areas? Which ones have become much more important to you and why? Which ones are still less important or seemingly out of reach? Why?

3. The Pauline paraphrase of Emerson's poem at the end of this chapter gives a three-part definition of success based on Philippians 4:12, 13 and 19. Which of these verses do you plan to make more effective in your life? How will you do this?

Thanks, Lord, for true success

Thanks for teaching me to be content in any situation . . . giving me strength to do whatever you ask me to . . . meeting all my needs in Christ Jesus.

Notes
1. Robert J. Ringer, *Looking Out for #1* (New York: Fawcett, Div. of Random House, 1978), p. 10.
2. Helen Gurley Brown, *Having It All* (New York: Pocket Books, Div. of Simon & Schuster, Inc., 1982).
3. Michael Korda, *Success!* (New York: Random House, 1977), pp. 4,5.
4. Denis Waitley, *Being the Best* (Nashville, TN: Thomas Nelson Publishers, 1987), p. 205.
5. Ibid.
6. From Walter A. Heiby, *Live Your Life* (New York: Harper and Row, Publishers, 1964, 1965 and 1966).
7. Harold Kushner, *When All You've Ever Wanted Isn't Enough* (New York: Summit books, 1986), p. 22.
8. Ibid., p. 23.
9. W. E. Vine, *Vine's Expository Dictionary of Old and New Testament Words* (Old Tappan, NJ: Fleming H. Revell Co., 1981), p. 279.
10. William Barclay, *The Letter to the Philippians, Colossians, Thessalonians, The Daily Study Bible* (Edinburgh: The St. Andrew Press, 1959), pp. 103,104.